oadStreet Publishing® Group, LLC
vage, Minnesota, USA
oadStreetPublishing.com

ourage to Conquer: 365 Devotions from Joshua, Judges, and Ruth
opyright © 2022 Brian Simmons

78-1-4245-6366-1 (faux leather)
78-1-4245-6367-8 (e-book)

less indicated otherwise, all Scripture quotations are from The
ssion Translation®. Copyright © 2017, 2018, 2020 by Passion
Fire Ministries, Inc. Used by permission. All rights reserved.
ePassionTranslation.com.

ck or custom editions of BroadStreet Publishing titles may be
rchased in bulk for educational, business, ministry, fundraising,
sales promotional use. For information, please email
ders@broadstreetpublishing.com.

ver and interior by Garborg Design Works | garborgdesign.com

Printed in China

22 23 24 25 26 5 4 3 2 1

Courage

TO

Conquer

365

DEVOTIONS
FROM JOSHUA,
JUDGES, AND
RUTH

BRIAN SIMMO

BroadStreet
PUBLISHING

Dedication

To all the faithful servants of Jesus
who have overcome passivity
and stand faithful in difficult times of pressure
this book is lovingly dedicated.

Introduction

A new beginning stretches out before you! Today you will embark on a journey into your own personal "promised land." Christ himself will be your Guide and King. You will find yourself going from one triumph to the next when you follow the Mighty King, Jesus. When we read the book of Joshua, we learn the ways of God: how he moves us forward, how we triumph over our enemies, and how we do the impossible. Joshua, a former slave in Egypt, became the leader of God's people after the death of Moses. A generational transfer took place as a younger generation rose with fresh vision, bold faith, and renewed passion to possess all that God had given them. All this and more is contained in the book you have in your hand, *Courage to Conquer*.

Just as Joshua had to face new challenges, so will you face challenges in your journey deeper into your promised land. There are giants, daunting enemies who are committed to hindering you and keeping you from your inheritance. Giants of fear, intimidation, insecurity, and helplessness—but *you* will have courage to conquer each one when Jesus is at your side.

How we need courage today to move forward in spite of the tests and trials we face! The courage of our heavenly Joshua (Jesus) is available for you today. It's time to shake off passivity and put on the new garments of faith and courage. Your wilderness wandering is now over. It's time to move forward. The old things that once sustained you may not be as helpful as they once were. The new has come. Manna has ceased; the Jordan is behind you. And new beginning has opened up before you. Take courage, my friend, the Mighty God is with you!

I pray that each one who takes this journey of reading a daily portion from *Courage to Conquer* will be empowered to overcome every opposition and every foe that may hinder your advance in God. Don't stop believing, don't stop moving forward, even if your progress seems slow. The Lord is with you to conquer, so be bold and courageous. Watch your "city walls" fall. Nothing can stand before you when Jesus lives in you!

God bless you, my friend,

Brian Simmons

New Beginning

After Moses, Yahweh's servant, died,
Yahweh spoke to Joshua son of Nun,
Moses' faithful assistant.

JOSHUA 1:1

As the book of Joshua opens, we find Israel in the midst of a transition between the old era under Moses and the beginning of a new one, with a new leader and prophet of Israel, Joshua. Joshua had been Moses' faithful assistant after the pilgrimage out of Egypt when Israel wandered in the wilderness. No doubt, there was grief around the death of Moses. He had led the people out of their captivity. He had met with God and passed on the Ten Commandments to the people. He had been the frontrunner to whom Israel looked. And yet, amidst Israel's mourning, God raised up another leader over them. A new beginning was before them when they would finally enter into their promised land.

Is there an ending that you are grieving? Has a door closed in an area of your life? Even in your mourning, you are not without hope. God has his steady hand upon your life. He will continue to direct you, and he will not fail to guide you into greater goodness.

Yahweh, even in my grief, I turn to you. Speak to me and encourage my heart in your wonderfully wise purposes. I trust you to guide me still.

MOVE AHEAD

"My servant Moses is dead. Now get up!
Prepare to cross the Jordan River, you and all the people.
Lead them into the land that I am giving to the Israelites."

JOSHUA 1:2

What is the Lord speaking over you today? Is there an area of your life where you have felt stuck without the breakthrough you have been longing for? The mercy of God moves us forward. We do not have to feel ready. We don't have to have all the details figured out. When God tells us to prepare ourselves for the journey ahead, let's take him at his word and make obedience our reply.

When God tells us that it is time to move ahead, we can be sure that as our loyal and loving leader, he goes with us. Trust that the one who is calling you forward will prepare the way ahead of you. He will be with you, and he will continue to provide you with all you need for the journey. His faithfulness is sure. When God's timing is right, it is the right time to move. Listen to what the Lord is saying and respond in faith.

Lord, speak to me like you spoke to Joshua. I want to hear your clear voice directing me out of my wandering ways. I will follow you.

LAND OF PROMISE

"Every part of the land where you march I will give you,
as I promised Moses."

JOSHUA 1:3

God's promises are his vow, and his vow is backed up by his unshakable character. The one who is overflowing in loyal love is the same one who leads us into our victory. What promises of God have you built your life upon? How many of those are still in the process of being fulfilled? Though we cannot know God's timing, we can rest in the faithfulness of his nature. What he says, he will do. What he speaks, he will follow through on.

Wherever you are, God is with you. Wherever you go, he will be with you still. Cling to him above all else, and you will know the overwhelming peace of his presence. Take confidence in who he is, no matter the unknowns before you. He is steady in love, he is able to deliver you from your fears and your enemies, and he will do what he has promised to do. Lean on him, for he is your ever-present help. Trust his Word and keep moving forward into the land of promise.

Unchanging One, I trust your mercy more than I do my own understanding. Walk with me, instruct me, lead me, and draw me closer to you today.

FRESH VISION

"Your borders will extend from the southern desert to the northern mountains of Lebanon, and from the great river Euphrates in the east, to the Mediterranean in the west."

JOSHUA 1:4

*H*ave you ever felt as if you exhausted God by needing reminders of what he has already spoken? Thankfully, he does not grow tired of answering our questions. He does not withhold information or shame us for our faulty memories. He is incredibly and wonderfully patient with us.

Spend time in the presence of the Lord and ask him to speak directly to your heart. He knows what you need to hear; he knows the encouragement you need. He has plans for you, and he will not keep them to himself. He clearly gave Joshua the borders of Israel's promised land, and he will show you the parameters of your own. When you know what is yours, you can confidently walk in the promises of God. Press in and hear what the Spirit is saying.

Spirit, I ask you to speak directly to my heart today. Give me fresh vision for what is ahead and speak in specific ways that give clear borders to what has felt ambiguous up until now. I trust you!

WORD OF PROMISE

"Joshua, no one will be able to defeat you
for the rest of your life!
I will be with you as I was with Moses,
and I will never fail nor abandon you."

JOSHUA 1:5

How often have you heard that God would never fail or abandon you? Has it become a stale phrase in your mind, or does it still move you with the marvelous mercy that lies within its promise? Though the Lord was speaking directly to Joshua in this passage, these same words are invoked by the writer of Hebrews (13:5).

God promises that he will never fail. He cannot go against his merciful nature and take back a vow that he has made. *He will never fail. He will never abandon us.* When we look to Jesus, we can know that we are looking to the Faithful One. The Father and Son have given us their Spirit and promised that we will never be alone. No matter what we have done or what circumstances we find ourselves in, when we turn to God and look to him, we will find that he is nearer than we realized.

Faithful One, reveal yourself to me through your presence. Give me revelation to see where you are already working and give me the peace of your presence.

FROM CONVICTION TO ACTION

> "You must remain very strong and courageous!
> Be faithful to obey all the teaching
> that my servant Moses commanded you to follow...
> so that you will have overwhelming success
> in everything you undertake."
>
> JOSHUA 1:7

There is a reason why moving into the realm of God's promises requires courage. We do not walk forward into unknown territory able to rely on the limits of our past experiences. As we enter into new territory, there is an opportunity for expansion—of experience, of understanding, and of trust. There is no formula for success, only obedience to God's Word.

The Word of God is living and active. It is through Jesus that we know the Father, and Jesus is the Living Word made flesh. As we look through the lens of the Old Testament, may we do it with eyes that look for glimpses of Jesus in it. We need to rely on the Spirit of God to instruct us, to lead us, and to strengthen us with bold courage! As we align our lives with his kingdom ways, we walk in the light of his presence. This requires the empowering grace of his Spirit with us. Let us never stop looking to him for all that we need, for he is our source and our strength.

Spirit of God, give me the courage I need to keep following your loving lead. I trust you more than any other—including my own senses.

MEDITATE ON THE WORD

"Recite this scroll of the law constantly.
Contemplate it day and night and be careful
to follow every word it contains;
then you will enjoy incredible prosperity and success."

JOSHUA 1:8

There is so much wisdom found in the Word of God. When we meditate on God's ways, on his Word, and on his character, our minds transform with increased trust in his faithfulness. He has given us instructions for how to stay close to him and how to walk in the ways of his kingdom. He knows that we need his help and his direction, and we have it!

May you find encouragement and powerful transformation as you walk in the ways of God. Fix your eyes on Jesus, the one who reveals the very heart of your Father in heaven. Fellowship with the Spirit who is full of the fruit of peace, patience, kindness, gentleness, and so much more. Meditate on the Word of God, both written and spoken. Let it challenge, embolden, and mold you. There is power in the revelation of God!

Faithful One, as I ponder your Word, reveal your characteristics to me more and more. Let me see your faithfulness and your loyal love as my foundation. I long to know you more.

NO REASON TO FEAR

"I repeat, be strong and brave!
Do not yield to fear nor be discouraged,
for I am Yahweh your God,
and I will be with you wherever you go!"

JOSHUA 1:9

When we look at the reasons God gives us to not give in to discouragement or fear, we catch a glorious glimpse of his goodness. He tells us to be strong in his love, to be brave in his presence. There is no reason to let fear overtake us, for God is with us. He is the one who goes with us into every battle. He is our strength, our support, and our constant help.

There truly is no need to let worry paralyze us when we live in the reality of his presence. He does not leave us or abandon us. He does not take breaks, and he never slumbers. He is always aware of what is going on both in and around us. We can be confident in his clarity and encouraged in his ability to save, redeem, and restore. There is nothing that he cannot do. He is the God who splits seas, he is the Defender of the weak, and he is with you and me.

Yahweh, make your presence known to me. Encourage me in your strength and calm my anxious heart.

No More Wandering

"Go through the camp and instruct the people, 'Pack your bags; for within three days you will cross the Jordan to conquer and occupy the land that Yahweh your God is giving you to possess.'"

JOSHUA 1:11

Can you imagine what it was like for the Israelites who had been wandering in the wilderness for decades to be told that the time had come to move into the promised land? Much of the old generation had already passed away. Some of the Israelites had only known the desert life. And yet, here was Joshua telling them to pack their bags because God was giving them access to their long-awaited land.

There comes a point for each of us where God moves us from our wilderness wandering into the promises he has spoken over us. He does not demand that we take action on the spot, but he gives us time to pack our bags and ready ourselves. Is there a shift in season for you? What do you need to take with you into the next steps? Take some time and ask the Lord to show you.

God, thank you for the promise of a hopeful future. I want to walk with wisdom when entering a new season. Give me guidance as to what to leave behind and what to bring.

COVENANT OBEDIENCE

"Remember the words that Yahweh's servant Moses
commanded you: 'Yahweh your God is giving you this land.'"

JOSHUA 1:13

When Joshua spoke these words of Moses to the Israelites, he was reminding them of God's promise to them. Who of us does not need a reminder of what God has already said and done? It is good to remember what it is that he has spoken, along with the evidence of his faithfulness to the previous generations, in order to strengthen ourselves in the confidence of God's promises.

Take some time to go through the words that the Lord has spoken to you through the years. Refresh yourself in his goodness. Remind yourself of what God has said and what he has already done for you. If you have old journals, dig them out. If you have a record of prophetic words that were spoken over you, go back through them. As you do, may you be encouraged by the beauty of God's covenant and his generous love toward you.

My God, may I not forget what you have already spoken. May your faithfulness shine through my memories as I go over them with you. I will continue to follow you. Your loyal love draws me in time and time again. Be glorified in my life as I live yielded to your heart.

HOLY TRANSITIONS

"Therefore, your wives, your little ones, and your livestock may remain here, but all your valiant warriors must cross over with us armed."

JOSHUA 1:14

In seasons of transition, we may have to move in ways we haven't before. We may need to sacrifice time that we cherished previously in order to enter what God is calling us into. There will be times of rest and refreshing, and there will be times to press on in perseverance, eyes fixed on a goal.

Is there an area of life that is in transition? If so, be encouraged that you are not alone in it. Knowing the season you are in will help you to prioritize your time, energy, and attention. Take a moment with the Lord today and let him speak his words of wisdom over you. If you need direction, look to him. If you need a solution to a problem, he's got the answers. He has given you tools in this life, and more than that, you have his Spirit. As you move ahead, the Lord is with you in loyal leadership every step of the way.

Good Father, thank you for leading me in love no matter where I go. I trust you to guide me in the transitions of my life. Give me greater clarity as I look to you. I depend on you!

ROADMAP TO VICTORY

"They will take the lead and help their brothers until they take possession of the land that Yahweh your God is giving them as their homeland."

JOSHUA 1:14–15

*T*he life and power you are looking for is in the presence of God. Almighty God goes with you into every situation—every classroom and every board room. What God calls you to, he will equip you for. His Spirit is your constant and never-ending supply. The Spirit of God is your very life-source.

When you wonder which way to go, know that God is the one who leads you into victory. Look to him more than to any other. He will show you the way to go. And don't forget to help your brothers and sisters. Our God is the faithful help of the weak, and he is the loyal Advocate of the vulnerable. We are never meant to go through battles in this life alone. We are not one-man armies, but we are a family of God meant to help, encourage, and strengthen one another.

Gracious God, forgive me for the times when I have been overly concerned with building my own kingdom instead of yours. Give me eyes to see where others could use a helping hand and strengthen me in your steadfast love to love others well.

RENEWED PASSION

They answered Joshua: "We will do everything you have told us
and will go wherever you send us. We always obeyed Moses,
and we will always obey you."

JOSHUA 1:16–17

When Joshua spoke to the Israelites on behalf of Yahweh,
directing them forward in their faith, they responded with
reverence and respect. This kind of respect did not include just
their honor but also their obedience. They had seen God lead
Israel through Moses, and they recognized that Joshua could do
the same.

Joshua as a frontrunner is a revelation of Jesus. Jesus is our
heavenly leader, the one who guides us into the promises of
God in our lives. Do you need renewed passion? Do you need a
refreshing vision of his loyalty and love? Look to Jesus today, and
you will find that he has something to share with you for where
you are right now. He is faithful to lead you with his peace, and
you can always trust that his intentions for you are full of his mercy.
Will you go where he sends you?

*Jesus, I look to you as my leader and help. Where you send me,
I will go. What you say, I will do. Where you lead, I will follow.
Speak to me today!*

UNSUSPECTED HELP

The king sent messengers to Rahab, who said to her: "Turn over the men who entered your house. They're here to spy out our land." But Rahab had already hidden the two men.

JOSHUA 2:3–4

*M*ay we never judge a person's worth by what they do. God did not keep Rahab, a prostitute, from being named in the lineage of Jesus after she showed tremendous faith and courage by hiding within her home the spies from Israel. God honored her because of her tenacity and faith.

God sees our hearts, and he often works through the most unlikely sources. Just as God used Rahab to help Israel capture Jericho, he will also use any willing heart to further his purposes. None of us is disqualified from his great grace. He is the God who lifts up the humble. He is the one who honors the willing, no matter how the world perceives them. May we honor others in the same way, living lives yielded to God's great love.

God, thank you for using those who are willing, no matter what they look like. I align my heart with yours, laying down my own ideas of what makes a person worthy. You are the one who does great things, and I will follow your loving lead.

YAHWEH'S RENOWN

"As soon as we heard it, our hearts melted with fear, and we were left with no courage among us because of you. Yahweh, your God, is the true God who rules in heaven above and on earth below."

JOSHUA 2:11

What a beautiful statement of faith this is! Rahab described her reaction to the news of what Israel's God had done for them. She recognized his great power over heaven and earth, and she declared him as the ruler of all.

Can you recall a time when you heard of God moving in a miraculous act of mercy toward his people? Can you remember what you felt at the mention of his power? God still moves in magnificent ways through the work of his Spirit. He heals those who are sick, mends the brokenhearted, opens deaf ears, and makes blind eyes see. There is nothing he cannot do. Take some time to declare the greatness of God and ask him for more revelation of his incredible might today.

Great God, when I think about how you've moved, I am in awe. Do it again, Lord! Move in mighty miracles and lead us further into the liberty of your love.

ACTS OF KINDNESS

"Please, solemnly swear to me by the name of Yahweh
that you will show kindness to my family
because I have shown kindness to you."

JOSHUA 2:12

We cannot separate God's power from his kindness. His lavish love is clearly displayed through Jesus, the living image of the Father. Jesus instructed us to treat others the same way we want to be treated, to lay down our lives in love, and to yield our lives to God. Rahab did all these things in her great act of generosity and good faith. She recognized that Yahweh was greater than any other god, and she chose to risk it all for his sake.

When we choose to be kind to others, even at our own expense, it is never without a return. God sees it all, and he honors every movement we make in love. He certainly honored Rahab's risk. It is important that we recognize that kindness does not mean remaining comfortable. Love is risky, but it is worth it every time.

Yahweh, I want to reflect your love through the way I live and relate to others. Empower me to love others the way that you do, counting the cost and going the distance.

PLEDGES OF HONOR

The men answered, "If you don't disclose our mission to anyone, we'll pledge our lives for yours. Then, when Yahweh gives us this land, we'll honor our promise and treat you kindly."

JOSHUA 2:14

It is no small thing to pledge your life for another. It is not a trivial matter to make a promise of peace and then follow through on it. In this moment we read about in Joshua, Rahab was desperate. She risked her life in order to protect spies from an enemy army. All she asked in return was that she and her family would be shown the same kindness.

The response of the men was to promise to protect her if she would continue to follow through with her part. When she did, they were honor-bound to keep their vow. Are you someone whose word is trustworthy? Can others count on you to follow through on your promises? May the Lord strengthen and help you where you falter, and may he honor you in the areas where you are being faithful.

Trustworthy One, thank you for being reliable in mercy. I'm so glad to know that your word is your vow, and you never break it. I want to be more like you in this way. Transform me as I continue to move toward you in my choices.

THE CRIMSON ROPE

"When our invasion begins, bring all your family together in your house—your father and mother, your brothers and sisters...tie this crimson rope in the same window through which you let us down."

JOSHUA 2:18

The crimson rope that Rahab threw down from her window is a picture of our salvation through the blood of Christ. It is an emblem of faith that points us to Jesus. Rahab's salvation was signaled through the crimson rope, and ours is signaled through the crimson blood of Christ's sacrifice. What a wonderfully powerful image and foreshadowing this is!

No matter what our house has been used for, if we yield our lives to Yahweh, then his blood covers our shame. He uses willing hearts, and he marks us as his own. Let's live as those who are under his banner of love. He sets us free to dwell in the victory that he has already accomplished through the cross. He is our Savior, and we must rely on his help more than we rely on the fortresses of our own making. His promises are surer than the confidence of any person, city, or nation.

Redeemer, thank you for your blood that covers me and sets me free. You are my liberator, and I come alive in your mercy.

HE GOES BEFORE

"Yahweh has certainly handed over the entire land into our hands! All the people of the land melt in fear before us!"

JOSHUA 2:24

The great fame of Yahweh spread quickly through the land where God was leading Israel before God's people even approached its cities. The inhabitants of the land had heard about the great miracles that accompanied Israel, including the parting of the Red Sea when they left Egypt. They heard how Israel defeated famously strong kingdoms.

When you are facing situations that require courage, know that your God goes before you. His power and glory are on display for all to see, whether in the wilderness or in lands of plenty. Encourage yourself in your history with God. Build yourself up in the faithfulness of your Father. The same God who dried up the bed of the Red Sea for the Israelites to walk across is the same God who makes a way for you. The one who provided refuge to the Hebrew spies in Jericho will also provide shelter when you need it. He is worthy of your trust.

Yahweh, thank you for going before me in my battles. Thank you for leading me into your victory. Encourage my heart in your faithfulness as you remind me of what you have already done.

HOLY ANTICIPATION

Joshua was up bright and early the next morning. They broke camp, and Joshua led the Israelites from Acacia to the eastern bank of the Jordan. There they set up camp and waited until they crossed over.

JOSHUA 3:1

*V*ery rarely do we rush right into a promising situation where our dreams become reality. Usually there is a waiting period, whether it is a few days, months, or years. This time is precious, and we should not waste it. There is purpose in the preparation, and there is anticipation that builds in the time between the now and the not yet.

Don't be discouraged if you have taken forward movement and have found yourself at a standstill shortly after. Ask the Lord for his wisdom. It could just be that you are in the moment where you must camp and wait until you cross over the Jordan into your promised land. Don't despair; rather, celebrate the coming victory! Let holy excitement rise as you prepare yourself for the next steps. They will take faith, trust, and courage. Do not despise the waiting, for it is the place where you will launch into your destiny.

Holy Lord, give me your perspective of my present season. Help me to see where I am and what you are doing. Give me vision of the future and purpose in the preparation.

EYES ON THE ARK

"Watch for the priests of the tribe of Levi to lift the ark
of the covenant of Yahweh your God. When it starts moving,
follow it so you'll know which way to go, since you've never
marched this way before."

JOSHUA 3:3–4

The ark of the covenant was where the Israelites believed the manifest presence of God dwelt. It is a wonderful picture of Jesus Christ, for the power of Christ within us is what enables us to cross over into our full inheritance. Jesus is the one who leads us into it—he is our forerunner! With eyes fixed on him, we follow where he leads us. We go where he goes.

In the unknowns of this life, we have a way forward. Jesus Christ, our sure and steady hope of glory, resides within us through the presence of his Spirit. He is the vision that directs us, the one who keeps us in place when we would wander on our own, and the confidence we need when stepping outside of our comfort zones. He always knows the way, so let's look to him.

My God, I look to you for vision, for direction, and for hope. Show me the way to go, and I will walk in it. When you move, I will move. Lead me, Lord.

GET YOURSELF READY

Joshua instructed the people, "Get yourselves ready!
Set yourselves apart for Yahweh! Tomorrow,
Yahweh will perform for us great miracles!"

JOSHUA 3:5

*H*ave you ever considered what it means to set yourself apart for God? In worship, we need both whole-hearted devotion and heart purity. What does it look like to sanctify ourselves before the Lord? Let us not simply go through the outward motions of worshiping God when we're around other believers and then living as we please the rest of the time.

If our hearts are not engaged in humble love before the Lord, he knows it. We could look like the holiest of Christians with our actions, and yet if we harbor hatred in our heart, we miss the whole point. We cannot fool God. Let us yield our hearts to him, letting his mercy change us from the inside out. His love transforms us. When we humble ourselves before the Lord, he will lift us up. He will lead us on his miraculous path of victory.

Great God, I ready myself in your presence, and I offer you access to every part of my heart and life. Transform me by your love and lead me in your mercy!

BLESSED ASSURANCE

> "This is how you will know for sure that the Living God
> is among you. As you advance into the land,
> he will drive out before you the Canaanites."
>
> JOSHUA 3:10

God is active in the lives of his children. He guides us, giving us clues of his kindness and cues of his faithfulness. When we feel alone in our battles, may we look to see where God is driving out our enemies before us. Let's keep pushing forward where he has already shown us to go, for that is where we will witness the miracles of his marvelous mercy.

What proverbial land are you advancing into? Keep your eyes ahead and ask God to show you where he is already working to clear the way. He does not grow weary in helping you. He does not tire of answering your questions. Press into him, even as you move forward toward the unknowns of your future. Do what you already know to do and rely on him to show you the rest as you move in him.

Living God, thank you for the reassurance of your presence with me as I venture into the unknowns of my future. I trust you to do what I could never achieve on my own. You are my God, and I am your child.

LORD OF ALL THE EARTH

> "Look! The ark of the covenant of the Lord of all the earth will go before you and prepare a way for you through the Jordan."
>
> JOSHUA 3:11

The raging waters of the river Jordan were yet another invitation for a miracle of Yahweh to lead his people through on dry land. Who is like the God who peels back rushing river tides to present a dry path for his people? God has not changed since then. He is still the Lord of all the earth, and every command he gives the wind and waves is obeyed.

Is the Lord leading you into a seemingly impossible situation? Is his presence pulling you in a direction that is unfamiliar and yet requiring you to trust him? The Israelites remembered what Yahweh had done in the Red Sea, and here he was doing it again. Will you trust that God will faithfully provide for you as you follow him? Put your confidence in him, for he is the same all-powerful God. He does not play tricks on his people, and he will not abandon you to be overtaken by the tides.

Lord of all the earth, prepare a way to walk where I can see none. I know where I am and where you are calling me. Make a way through!

GREAT MIRACLE

"The moment the feet of the priests carrying the ark of Yahweh...
touch the water of the Jordan, a great miracle will happen!
The water flowing downstream toward you will stop and pile up
as if behind a dam."

JOSHUA 3:13

The ways of the Lord are not our ways. He moves in mighty acts
of wonder, clearing a path in the overflowing floodwaters of our
lives. If we will follow him, we will be amazed at what Yahweh
does. As we surrender our lives to his ways, he leads us through
impossible situations with miracle provisions.

As we follow the Lord, he makes a way. Let's not linger on the
shores of our dreams and his promises when he is already clearing
a path ahead of us. He does not lead us into destruction but into
the abundance of his love. No matter what awaits us on the other
side, let's trust God to guide us into his goodness. He is faithful,
and he will not fail. He is the God of miracles!

*Faithful Lord, I trust you to lead me with your power. I set my eyes
on you, for you are my confidence. May my eyes not wander from
you, for you are my hope and the one who sustains me.*

CROSSING OVER

Yahweh completely cut off the flow of the river so that it drained downstream toward the Desert Sea...So the people crossed over opposite Jericho...The entire nation passed by the ark as they completed their miracle-crossing on dry ground.

JOSHUA 3:16–17

*W*hen the Lord moves, he does not move us. He requires us to pursue him. He leads; we follow. He speaks; we respond in obedience. If we wait for God to do our part, we will waste our lives away. A living relationship is not one-sided. It takes both parties giving and receiving. Do we approach our relationship with God in the same way?

Surely the mercy of God goes before us. This crossing was not a surprise to the nation of Israel. God had already told them through Joshua what to expect. What has God spoken to you? Don't be surprised when the time comes, and it requires steps forward in faith. Don't hesitate to respond when he moves. Recall what he has already said and follow him as you cross over into a new land.

Yahweh, thank you for your leadership in my life. Increase my faith as I follow after you. I will respond to your words of life with hope in my heart and trust in your faithfulness.

STONES OF REMEMBRANCE

"The stones will always be a sign to you...
These stones will serve as a memorial for Israel forever."

JOSHUA 4:6–7

After Israel crossed the Jordan on dry land, Joshua instructed one man from each tribe to go to where the ark of the covenant was in the middle of the riverbed and to each bring back one stone. There, on the shore of the Jordan, Joshua set up the memorial stones to serve as a reminder of the miracle-crossing for Israel.

Perhaps you have experienced a great deliverance in your life. Where has God moved mightily on your behalf? Consider how you can build a memorial to this memory. Is there a reminder that you can keep that will serve to encourage you through the remembrance of God's goodness toward you? Be creative with how you go about this. It does not have to be a literal stone, but let it connect you to the experience you walked through with God's guidance.

God of miracles, inspire my heart with creative ways to honor what you have done. When you lead me through impossible situations, help me to recall this beautiful act of making a memorial of remembrance.

FAVOR OF GOD

On that day, Yahweh exalted Joshua before all the people.
As they had stood in awe of Moses, so they stood in awe of Joshua
for the rest of his life.

JOSHUA 4:14

Joshua was not a perfect man, but he yielded his life to the Lord in surrender. He led the Israelites out of the wilderness into their inheritance. In the same way that God had been with Moses, he was with Joshua. And in the same way that the people were amazed by Moses and his relationship with God, so were they amazed by Joshua.

When we walk in surrender to the Lord and his ways, his favor is visible to others. He is our help, our guide, and our strength. Jesus has leveled the playing field so that everyone can know God as closely as the prophets of old. There is nothing that separates us from the love of God through his presence, for Jesus has broken down every barrier. Jesus himself is our favor before the Father and others. It is through him that we are led into freedom.

Exalted One, I give you access to every part of my life. I surrender to your will and your ways. May you be honored in my life even as you were honored in Joshua's.

LISTEN AND RESPOND

So Joshua did as he was commanded.

JOSHUA 4:17

In the presence of God, we find our peace and our purpose. We also find instruction and guidance. Do we take time to cultivate relationship with him, listening for his voice? When God speaks, how quick are we to respond? We will not know what to do, which way to go, or how to honor God if we do not spend time with him.

The more we get to know him, the more readily our hearts will receive his message. We know that this was not simply true of the Old Testament prophets and figures but of Jesus as well. He spent time with his Father in solitude. He prayed, and he sought direction. He said that he only did what he saw the Father doing. In the same way, as we grow in depth in our relationship with the Lord, when he speaks, we will respond with our lives.

Wonderful One, I am so thankful that you are accessible and not far away. I want to know you more. Teach me as I spend time with you. Refine me as I follow your lead. Have your way as I obey your Word. You are worthy of my pursuit and my very life.

FUTURE GENERATIONS

"In time to come, when children ask their fathers, 'Why are these stones so important?' tell them, 'Here is the place where the Israelites crossed the Jordan on dry ground!'"

JOSHUA 4:21–22

*O*ur testimonies are not for our own sake. The stories of God's faithfulness to us are not simply for our own encouragement but for future generations as well. When you think over your walk with the Lord, can you recall testimonies of his faithfulness? Do you spot his goodness toward you through his acts of mercy in your life?

Take some time in the presence of the Lord, asking him to bring to mind the faithfulness he has shown you in your history. As they come to mind, thank him. As you go about your day, find someone to share it with. You never know the encouragement and impact you may have on another. There is power in your story, and the Lord can move mightily through it.

Faithful Father, will you remind me of how you have moved in my life in specific and terrific ways? Will you show me, too, how you moved in previous generations within my family and region? I long to draw courage from what you have done and pass it on to others.

HEART CIRCUMCISION

Yahweh commanded Joshua, "Make knives of flint and circumcise the men of Israel again." So Joshua made stone knives and circumcised all the men.

JOSHUA 5:2–3

Circumcision was the sign of the covenant that God made with Abraham. The importance of Israel's circumcision before battle was the renewal of the covenant between God and Israel. The children who were born in the wilderness had not yet been circumcised. As they went through this procedure, it was symbolic of submitting their human nature to Yahweh so that they might enter into the fullness of their inheritance.

We, too, can learn from this. When we submit ourselves to Christ, we throw off the old ways of relying on our understanding, and we are free to live in the Spirit of God. We enter into the fullness of our spiritual inheritance. Is there a part of your life that you have kept from the Lord? Is there anything that has kept you from walking in the fullness of your freedom in Christ? Let Jesus, your heavenly heart surgeon, cut away the old so that you may walk into the new, freed up and ready to receive.

Yeshua, take my heart and cut away anything that keeps me from the fullness of your Spirit life. I yield myself to you, trusting your covenant ways.

February

WAIT ON HEALING

After the circumcision was completed,
the whole nation waited in the camp
until their wounds had healed.

JOSHUA 5:8

It is not wise to rush from wound to battle. After the Israelite men had been circumcised, they needed time to fully heal before they could move ahead. Do you sense a theme here? There was movement forward and then some days that followed when they needed to rest. This is not the first time in Joshua we see this pattern. There are rhythms of rest that may seem counterintuitive but are necessary to our success.

In a culture that values time as a commodity, it is difficult to see rest as necessary to our well-being and victory. It is high time that we shift our mindset about it. When we are wounded, we do ourselves no favors by pushing ourselves harder. If we take the necessary time to rest and recover, we will heal quicker. If we ignore our pain and rush ahead into battle, it only makes us vulnerable to defeat. May we be people who value the time it takes to heal.

Healer, thank you for the reminder of our need for rest and recuperation. I want to be a proponent of others' healing. May I be patient in love, just as you are, with myself and with others.

DISGRACE ROLLED AWAY

Then Yahweh said to Joshua, "Today, I have rolled away your disgrace from being slaves in Egypt." For that reason, the place is named Gilgal to this day.

JOSHUA 5:9

Jesus rolls away our disgrace with the covenant of his strong love. He washes over the pain of our past with the liquid mercy of his blood. The shame of our youth is not held against us, and the power of his love sets us free to venture into what he has for us in the great expanse of his glorious kingdom.

There is now no accusing voice of condemnation against those of us who are joined in life-union with Jesus (Romans 8:1). We have been liberated from our captivity, and we are free in Christ. What a beautiful invitation we have to live, move, and have our being in fellowship with the King of Kings. He leads us into his kindness, and he guides us with his presence. What a wonderful Savior!

Jesus, thank you for the ways that you were foreshadowed in the Old Testament. I long to know you more. Thank you for setting me free in your love and for removing my shame. I am undone by your wonderful mercy in my life.

REMEMBER TO FEAST

While encamped at Gilgal, not far from Jericho,
the Israelites celebrated the Feast of Passover in the
evening of the fourteenth day of the month of Abib.

JOSHUA 5:10

Just as memorial stones spoke to the faithful miracles of God, keeping the Feast of Passover was a chance for Israel to commemorate and celebrate their deliverance from slavery in Egypt. Leading up to their exodus, God moved in powerful ways. There was no lack of wonders that God performed for his people. This is true for us today too.

As we commemorate our own freedom from the confinement of shame and fear, whether through an anniversary of our submission to the Lord or through an act of gratitude in our fellowship with him, let's not forget the element of celebration. He led us out of our own captivity into his glorious freedom. There is so much to joyously thank God for doing in our lives, so let's not forget to feast on his goodness regularly.

Great God, thank you for leading me out from under fear's control. I am free in your love, and you have given me so much grace to move in. I celebrate my liberty with joy today!

FRUIT OF THE LAND

On that day, when they ate the produce of the land, the manna stopped falling from heaven. The Israelites never ate manna again, but that year they enjoyed the fruit of the land of Canaan.

JOSHUA 5:12

*E*very child is weaned from simple survival and sustenance on milk to solid foods as they grow. Spiritually, we also move from being hand-fed the simple truths of the gospel to eating the diverse fruit of the kingdom as we mature. When the Israelites moved from wilderness into the promised land, God no longer needed to feed them from heaven's manna, for they had the abundance of food in the land before them.

Perhaps you find yourself in a transition where provision looks different. When we learn to grab hold of what is in front of us and to feast on the bounty of new lands, it may seem as if God is not as involved in our provision. But this isn't so! We get to partner with his plans and purposes in new ways, relying as heavily on his leadership as we did before—it may simply look different.

Provider, thank you for leading me into new seasons where my growth does not threaten your sovereignty. Every time I enjoy the fruit of this season, I will give you praise!

COMMANDER OF YAHWEH'S ARMIES

"I have not come to take sides but to take charge.
I am the Commander of Yahweh's armies."

JOSHUA 5:14

*W*hen we encounter Jesus the way that Joshua encountered the Commander of Yahweh's armies, a few things happen. He asserts his lordship and leadership. He declares that he does not take sides, but he takes charge. We can trust him to lead us with the confidence of his mighty mercy and supernatural strength.

As we worship him in response, we give him our allegiance. When Jesus reveals himself to us, we cannot help but humble ourselves in reverence before him, for he is glorious and worthy of our submission. The places where God meets us with his presence also become holy ground. May we honor his presence by not rushing to move on. Let's take off our sandals and stay with him awhile. We will be strengthened, encouraged, and emboldened as we worship him in spirit and truth.

Jesus, you are the commander of my life. I yield to your leadership, and I worship you in your glory. I know that you are able to lead me into your victory, and I will walk with you into the endless triumph of your kingdom.

UNTOLD BLESSINGS

The Commander of Yahweh's armies said to Joshua,
"Remove your sandals, for you are standing on holy ground!"
And Joshua obeyed.

JOSHUA 5:15

The inheritance of Jesus that we partake in is more than the promises of provision, abundance, peace, victory over sin, and freedom from fear. It is unhindered fellowship with God. The Father, Spirit, and Son are unified in loving relationship. We, too, enter into freedom of communion with God through his Spirit when we submit our lives to Christ.

The untold blessings are far more than feasting on harvest fruit and fattened calves. They are worth more than gold, rubies, or pearls. The most sacred and most fulfilling blessings we receive happen as we fellowship Spirit to spirit. They are in relationship. They are in intimacy with God. In the new covenant of God's mercy through Christ's sacrifice, we experience the fullness of his love without barrier. There are no veils to separate us from the love of Christ. We stand on the holy ground of his presence meeting us where we are in the dirt. What wonderful news!

Christ Jesus, thank you for breaking down every barrier that kept us from your lavish love. I long to know you more. I worship you in humble adoration. You are wonderful!

FAITH TO SEE

Yahweh commanded Joshua, "See, I have given Jericho,
its king and mighty warriors into your hands."

JOSHUA 6:2

When Yahweh speaks, he calls us to a higher perspective. He invites us to see from his vantage point, with eyes of faith. Eyes of faith that look at an armored city and say it is as good as rubble. Eyes of faith that see a strong army and declare it defeated. We do not have to know the whole plan from the start. Our confidence is in God not in our own abilities and strategies.

When God says it is so, let's take him at his word. When he speaks triumph over overwhelming odds, let's believe him. The same God who formed the mountains can throw them into the sea. The one who filled the great deep can also drain the waters. May we look with eyes of faith, not with skeptical eyes of cynicism. Either way, God will follow through with faithfulness. Let's be found faithful to his ways and align ourselves in his mercy.

King of kings, I trust that your ways are higher than my ways and your thoughts are high above my own. I want to look from your vantage and see what you see. Open my eyes and increase my faith.

BEFORE YOUR EYES

"When you hear the blare of the shofars,
have all the people shout with a mighty shout of joy!
Then the walls of the city will collapse before your eyes."

JOSHUA 6:5

God's battle plans do not look like the strategies of human minds. He instructed the Israelites to march around the city walls several times—once a day for six days and seven times on the seventh day. At the end of the seventh march around the city walls, the shofars would blare, the people shout, and then the walls of the city would collapse.

Does this sound too fantastical to be true? Often, God's wonders do seem hard to believe. God regularly moves in mysterious ways to reveal his power through us. No humans could claim that they had caused the walls of the city of Jericho to crumble. It was God's battle plan, and it was his doing. His people were simply obedient and partnered with his plan. May we be people of great faith who follow his lead, no matter how bizarre it may seem.

Yahweh, I trust that your plans are better than my own. I want to see your power at work before my very eyes. I choose to partner with your will and ways.

WAIT FOR IT

> Joshua had commanded the rest of the people,
> "Do not shout! Remain silent! Don't make a sound
> until the moment I command you to shout."
>
> JOSHUA 6:10

When we follow God's instructions, we must not neglect his timing. Though we may know what to do, we must discern the right moment and wait for it. Rushing will not help us at all. Have you ever found yourself hastily running through the motions of something and then realized you made a mess of it because of your carelessness?

As we learn to practice patience in the walking out of God's promises, we will find that endurance serves us well. Patience is a fruit of the Spirit's work in our lives. He is not hasty, and he does not rush. Just as we cannot hurry our healing, so we cannot hasten the shout of victory until God says it is time. May we learn the beauty of abiding in the presence of God, not rushing to make his plans happen, but trusting that his timing is good and that he will not fail.

Wise One, I yield my heart to yours and trust your timing over my own. Though I want to move full steam ahead, help me to rest in your wisdom and move forward in your timing.

JOYFUL SHOUT

After their seventh time around, when the priests
were about to blow the shofars, Joshua commanded the people:
"Shout a shout of joy! Yahweh has given you the city!"

JOSHUA 6:16

Sometimes, our victory does not come by force but by
declaration. When God says that we are triumphant in his victory,
let's accept it as truth. May we shout for joy because God has
given us the victory—not in our own strength but by his.

Christ has given us victory over fear and shame. He has delivered
us from our captivity and now leads us into our inheritance in him.
There is abundance in his kingdom, there is joy in his presence,
and he is the one who always goes before us into every battle
we face. May we rely on his leadership and on his overcoming
strength more than we do our own ideas of success. His invitation
is for far greater things than we can imagine. Let's lift a joyful shout
as he leads us into his triumph.

*Jesus, you are the victorious One over all. You lead me into your
triumph, and I get to partake in the abundance of your kingdom.
Joy fills my heart. Thank you for your victory!*

DEVOTED OFFERING

"Jericho and everything in it
are to be a devoted offering to Yahweh."

JOSHUA 6:17

When God moves in our lives, how do we respond? Do we offer him what he deserves? Do we devote the offering of his goodness back to him? May we have wisdom and grace to walk humbly with him, surrendering all that he has given back to him.

When we hold too tightly to our ideas of God's promises, not willing to give him what he asks for, the resulting pain is our own doing. May we walk in his ways with open hands of submission. May we give him back the generosity of his gifts by following his loving lead. May we dedicate all that we have to the glory of God, reflected in his love. When we have the freedom to generously offer others what they need because we do not value our possessions above the law of God's love, we live like his images of compassion on the earth. All the earth, everything in it, belongs to him. Let's not forget it.

Yahweh, I devote all that you have given me to your glory and your fame. Use my life to generously reflect your loving-kindness as I give as you lead me to do.

INCREDIBLE VICTORY

They raised a massive shout of jubilee like a thunderclap,
and all at once the thick walls of Jericho collapsed!
Everyone rushed straight ahead and captured the city.

JOSHUA 6:20

*I*magine what it must have been like to march around the city
walls of Jericho multiple times over the span of a week. What must
it have felt like to be a part of a walking party with the citizens
of the city curiously watching on? When the time finally came to
let out a massive shout of jubilee, it was so overwhelming that it
caused the very walls of Jericho to collapse before them!

What joy they must have felt as the walls came tumbling down.
Imagine how the jubilee swelled and grew even stronger as they
realized that God was doing what he said he would do. May we
find our own joy growing as we walk in obedience to the Lord and
his Word over our lives. Then we will rush ahead into the victory
that he has already provided.

*Wonder-working Lord, who else can cause fortresses to crumble
with a unified shout? Is it not you who provides the victory we
need? I will follow you; I trust you more than the world's ways, for
you are faithful and true.*

TIME TO REPENT

But the Israelites violated the commandment regarding
the wealth of Jericho that was to be set apart for the Lord.

JOSHUA 7:1

*W*hen is the right time to repent? There is no "too soon" when it comes to contrition. May we be people who are quick to turn to the Lord when we have violated his law of love. Our devotion is not dependent on perfection—there is so much grace and mercy in the generous heart of God. He restores us when we turn to him.

Whenever we go off on our own way, thinking that we know better than Jesus, may we hear the correction of his voice and return to him. Let us surrender to his ways. God is not vindictive; he always moves in justice, in mercy, and in steady character. We may misunderstand his intentions, but that does not change his character; it simply changes our perception of who he is. Right now is the time to repent. Today is the day of restoration and renewal. May we seize it and not waste another moment.

Lord, forgive me for the ways I have broken my devotion to you. I surrender to your ways, and I turn from the error of my own. Wash over me with your mercy and cover the fault of my ways.

DISAPPOINTING DEFEAT

Joshua and the elders of Israel tore their clothes
and threw dust over their heads to show their sorrow.

JOSHUA 7:6

*N*ot every battle is victorious, and not every circumstance in
life is cause for celebration. There are times to weep and mourn.
There are seasons where we wrestle with our questions, and we
ask God for answers. Defeat is discouraging. Let's not be too
quick to move on from our sorrow when our hearts are grieved by
disappointment.

We do not wallow in our suffering, but we also should not
dismiss our reasons for mourning. There is joy ahead, as Isaiah
61 promises, but there is darkness before the light of dawn brings
relief. Are you acquainted with grief? Do you embrace it, or do
you try to brush off the pain of your loss? God does not dismiss
our hard feelings. Let's feel what we need to feel in order to truly
experience the depths of our disappointment. The Spirit is our
Comforter, and he is close in our suffering.

*Comforter, even when my pain is of my own doing, you draw near
in comfort. I will not turn away from the disappointment I feel. Be
with me in it and help me move through it to see the light you are
shining, even here in the midst of my discomfort.*

LAY OUT YOUR QUESTIONS

Joshua cried out, "O Lord Yahweh, why did you lead these people across the Jordan? To be defeated? To be killed by the Amorites?"

JOSHUA 7:7

The Lord over all welcomes our questions, even when they hold hints of accusation. He is not afraid of our authentic wrestling with the dissonance between our realities and God's promises. He can handle our honesty. May we bring him the fullness of our thoughts, our hard questions, and our hearts. It is better to wrestle with the Lord than it is to ignore our grief, disappointment, and confusion.

Yahweh does not turn us away when we look to him for answers—even if we lose our cool. He corrects our arrogance, our disobedience, and our false mindsets concerning his nature. However, he does not require us to be joyful when we are mourning a great loss. He does not expect us to figure out the solution to confusing dilemmas on our own. Don't be afraid to be honest with him. God may just use the opportunity to speak truth, healing, and restoration.

O Lord, I come to you with my honest questions, my discouragement, and my doubt. As I do, speak your words of life over me and change my heart.

PURIFY THE PEOPLE

"Get up and purify the people
in preparation for tomorrow."

JOSHUA 7:13

Sometimes, we need to clear the air and just get everything out on the table to make things right. There was sin in Israel's camp, and Joshua needed to deal with it. When there is something keeping our families, friends, or communities from thriving in love, we need to confront the areas of hidden compromise.

We begin with our own hearts. That is always the case. When we humble ourselves before God, he shines the light of his truth on our inner world and motivations. May we not rush to judge our brother or sister before we deal with our own areas of compromise. A people becomes purified as we each humble ourselves before God and before others.

Pure and Holy One, in the blood of Jesus I am cleansed. It is your righteousness that has become my own—thank you! Give me courage to be humble and honest in my faults and failures and how they've affected others. I don't want to have any hidden compromise in my heart or lifestyle. Purify me in your love.

A NEW DAY

Yahweh said to Joshua,
"Do not yield to fear nor shrink back because of Israel's failure...
See, I have handed over to you the city."

JOSHUA 8:1

*F*ailure is inevitable in our lives. We are not perfect humans, but we are perfected in Christ. He gives us new opportunities to move ahead when we have made a mess of things. What mercy! Though fear causes us to shrink back, the love of God propels us forward.

If you find yourself feeling beaten down by yesterday's failure, know that there is fresh mercy to meet you in the presence of your gracious God today. He will give you the strategies you need to move ahead in his strength. He is the God of second chances. Though there may have been sin in the camp, God's purposes are not prevented. Today is a new day—hear what the Lord is calling you into and walk in the confidence of his faithfulness toward you.

Yahweh, fill me with courage where regret has caused me to stand still. I want to follow you with confidence and trust in your unfailing character. Fill me with boldness as I go into this new day.

HEAVENLY ORDERS

"Now that you have your orders,
go and do as Yahweh has commanded!"

JOSHUA 8:8

God is living and active in this world and in our lives. He is not silent; he speaks to us through his Word and through his Spirit. Even as he moves in us, we are not simply to be "hearers" of the Word but also "doers" of the Word (James 1:22). When God speaks, we respond with obedience. Where he guides us, let us follow.

We can be sure that when God leads us out in his mercy, he will not abandon us along the way. Our confidence does not come from our own abilities, but from God's. He is our constant companion and our champion Defender. He gives us courage to conquer our fears as we follow his lead in our lives. Let us not let anything hold us back from walking out in confidence the orders that he has given us. The one who calls us is always faithful.

Faithful God, I willingly choose to follow you today. Give me boldness and strength to walk in faith and do what you have called me to do.

TRIUMPH OVER ENEMIES

Not a man remained in Ai or in Bethel who did not
go out in pursuit of Israel, leaving their city undefended.

JOSHUA 8:17

God is graciously working things together in his mercy, even when we cannot see. He draws out the obstacles to our victory and clears the way for us to overcome the barriers to our freedom. Let's not forget to lean on the wisdom of God. He doesn't leave out a detail, and we can trust him to tend to the particulars that we cannot anticipate.

Our combat is not a war against flesh and blood, as Ephesians 6:12 says. It is against rebellious spiritual principalities and authorities. Our battleground is in the place of prayer, in the act of love and mercy instead of vengeance. Belittling other people is not the way of Jesus. Let us never mistake the humanity of another for the enemy of our faith. Jesus gives us liberty in his love to overcome every stronghold. Let's trust him to do it.

Jesus, you are my leader and my victory. Without you, I have no direction. Looking to you, I see the vision of laid-down-love. As I follow you, lead me into greater liberty and triumph.

WORSHIP THERE

Afterward, Joshua built near Mount Ebal
a stone altar to Yahweh, the God of Israel.

JOSHUA 8:30

After the battle at Ai, Joshua led the people to a place outside of the city. There, he had a stone altar built to offer their sacrifice of praise to the God who had given them victory over their enemies. With the previous defeat still fresh in their minds, perhaps this victory felt even more wonderful. God clearly moved on their behalf.

When we experience the miracles of God's tangible mercy in our lives, it is appropriate to respond with worship. When he moves on our behalf, do we breathe a deep sigh of relief and then simply move on? Or do we take the time to honor God for what he alone could do in our lives? He moves in might, giving us the strength to conquer fear and to move ahead in wonderful ways. Let us take the time to worship him for his goodness toward us.

Yahweh, I'm so grateful for your leadership. I'm so thankful for what you've done. I worship you for the specific ways you've moved in my life, and I will keep on doing it.

STONE ALTAR

Moses had commanded them to build an altar
using stones that had not been cut with iron tools.
On it they offered to Yahweh burnt sacrifices
and fellowship offerings.

JOSHUA 8:31

The stone altar that Joshua built to honor Yahweh was
constructed in the same way that Moses had previously
commanded. The stones had not been cut with tools of the
people; this was meant to instruct the people in the power of God.
Salvation is only found through the mercy of God, not the work of
humankind. He alone made the ultimate altar, the cross of Jesus.

Nothing we could ever construct on our own gains us favor with
God. Our lives are the peace offerings we give to God in gratitude
for what he has done. We give them freely to him because of what
he has already done for us. We cannot add to or take away from
salvation through the mercy of Christ. He is the altar we lay our
lives down upon.

Savior, thank you for your acts of mercy throughout history.
Thank you for your active mercy in my life. I lay my life upon
the foundation of your salvation, for you are my hope. There is
nothing I hold back from you.

OBEY WRITTEN LAWS

Afterward, Joshua read aloud all the words of the law, the blessings and the curses, exactly as it was written in the scroll of the law. Joshua read aloud every word that Moses had commanded, and all the assembly of Israel heard it.

JOSHUA 8:34–35

Without law, would there be order? Imagine living in a lawless land, where anything goes. Where would the accountability be? What of justice? Though we may not agree with all the laws of the lands we inhabit, there is wisdom in following them. We know the consequences if we do not.

In the kingdom of God, there is also a semblance of law and order. God is wiser than the judges, kings, and priests of the earth. Though we have only glimpses of his understanding, he is far greater than us in our comprehension of the world and its ways. His ways are infinitely better than the ways of this world. If we follow the laws of earthly kingdoms, how much more should we live according to his principles?

Great God, thank you for your wisdom and your instruction. Thank you for the revelation of the wonder of your kingdom through Jesus. I choose to follow your ways, even when I don't understand the purpose of them.

COVERING OF COVENANT

When they arrived at Israel's camp at Gilgal, they said to Joshua and the Israelites: "We've come from a far country to propose that you make a treaty with us."

JOSHUA 9:6

The reputation of Israel went before them into neighboring cities and nations. Some responded by wanting to attack and defend; others responded with pleas of mercy. In this case, those in Gibeon sent out a delegation to garner a treaty of peace, but they disguised themselves as foreigners from a distant land.

God is a God of his word. Israel also reflected the importance of this in keeping a vow when they made it. Gibeon made a play for peace, albeit in a tricky way. Once Israel made a promise, they were bound to it. God is bound to the promises he makes. Not a single word he has spoken will return to him void. And he cannot be tricked, as the Israelites were. What he says he will do, he will do. Let's look to him and find the comfort and peace of his covenant with us through Christ.

Yahweh, thank you for your covenant of peace. Jesus, I am humbled in the great grace of your presence today. Encourage, strengthen, and love me to life in the garden of your peace.

CONSULT WITH GOD

The leaders of Israel ratified a peace treaty with the Gibeonites
by sharing a meal together, but they failed to consult with Yahweh.
Joshua agreed to let them live.

JOSHUA 9:14–15

*T*here will be times in our lives that we fail to consult with God.
Even in these times, there is grace. However, our choices have
consequences that we can't get rid of. God's mercy is large
enough to meet us where we are, to use even our mistakes for his
glory. But this does not mean that we should not look to him for
counsel and wisdom.

The consequences of our choices may affect our entire lives. We
cannot outrun them. Yet, God's love is large enough to carry us
through our responsibilities. His power is great enough to work all
things, even in our mistakes, to teach us, to mature us, and to lead
us further into leaning on him. Let's look to God for both the big
and the small decisions we face. He has wisdom to instruct us—
let's trust his perspective and take his Word seriously.

*God, I bring you my choices and the options I've been weighing.
Guide me in your wisdom and show me what I may be missing. I
trust you!*

THE LORD'S RENOWN

They answered Joshua, "We lied, sir, because we greatly feared
for our lives...We know for certain that Yahweh will honor his
promise to Moses and give you all these lands as your own."

JOSHUA 9:24

When God moves in power in our lives, people take notice. The
Gibeonites had heard of Yahweh's renown—of the great things that
he had done through Moses. They had heard of the promise that
God made Israel, and they were convinced that it would come
to pass. Their desperation led them to dishonesty, but it was their
very desperation that saved their lives.

How often do we come to God feeling at a loss? We may have
heard of what he has done for others. We may have experienced
his saving grace ourselves. Are we those who walk closely with
the Lord? Or are we those that have heard of what he has done
and are looking for mercy? Either way, we are not turned away
when we come to him. His peace has become our peace through
Jesus Christ.

*Great God, I have heard what you have done in ages past. I have
watched you move in the lives of others. I want to know your
power for myself. Jesus, you are my covering and my peace. Move
in my life!*

MARVELOUS MERCY

Joshua had mercy and saved them
from being killed by the Israelites.

JOSHUA 9:26

*I*n the history of Israel and doctrine of typology, Joshua is a
theological type of Jesus. Just as Joshua had mercy and saved
the Gibeonites from Israel's anger, Jesus has mercy on us. He has
delivered us from retribution. He is our safe place and Defender.
He is our gracious King who covers us in his covenant of love. He
does not break his vow; once sealed, it is unbreakable. It is our
eternal shield.

The blood of Jesus is the seal of his covenant with us. His
marvelous mercy is found in the laying down of his very life for all
who would come to him for shelter, for restoration, and for hope.
He is better than Joshua, he is better than Moses, and he is better
than Abraham. Jesus is the fullness of God in human form. He is
the Son, and he is the heir of all creation. What he says goes. His
mercy covers us forever.

*Merciful One, thank you for your unending love that has freed me
from the curse of sin and death. You are my life, and in you I am
completely covered by compassion. I am so grateful.*

VOW OF VICTORY

Yahweh spoke to Joshua: "Do not fear
the Amorite kings and their armies,
for I have decreed your victory over them;
not one will withstand you!"

JOSHUA 10:8

What God has decreed is backed by the assurance of his faithfulness. As we walk out in obedience to his word over our lives, the vow of his victory leads us in confidence. Fear is not our master. Jesus is. Let us take seriously the promises of God. Let's walk in faith, following the loving and victorious lead of our King Jesus.

There is power in the spoken word of God over our lives. We find courage when we need it, conviction by his Spirit, and strength to walk in his ways. What has God spoken over your life? Is there an area that you have been holding back in obedience because of fear? Bring it to the Lord and let him shine his light of truth on it. He will show you the way to go, and he will fill you with the peace of his presence as he instructs your heart.

Yahweh, when you promise victory, may I walk in the confidence of your faithfulness. I don't want to waver. I want to be strong in your Spirit-strength. Clothe me in your wisdom and flood me with your peace.

DIVINE HELP

Yahweh empowered Joshua and his army to chase them...Yahweh
hurled large hailstones on them from the sky...more men died
from Yahweh's hailstones than by the swords of the Israelites.

JOSHUA 10:10–11

*G*od gives us fresh courage to face our challenges. He
empowers us by the strength of his Spirit and gives us supernatural
energy, vision, and victory. The Lord himself fights for us and with
us. He clears a path, and he overpowers the tactics of the enemy.

The unparalleled power of Jesus goes with us into our trials and
troubles. He moves in awe-inspiring ways. May we take courage
in his help. He is greater than any force that opposes us. Jesus
overcame the grave, so nothing can hold him. Death could not
keep him, and certainly nothing that we face intimidates him. Let's
look to Jesus, our Warrior King, who goes with us into our battles
and who conquers every foe.

*King Jesus, I depend on your divine help to fight for me. I am
going where you lead me, so don't hold back your aid. You are my
courage, my strength, and the very hope of my life.*

March

GOD FOR US

It was the day Yahweh himself fought for Israel!
There has never been a day like it before or since—
a day when Yahweh obeyed the voice of a man!

JOSHUA 10:14

*W*hat a beautiful picture this is of the way that Christ fights for us. God responded to our need for mercy with his own Son. Jesus made a way through the wilderness of fear, shame, sin, and doubt and tore the veil that kept us from the fullness of God. God, who himself fought for Israel, is the same God who fights for our freedom.

Let's trust God with all that we cannot control. Let's follow him into the wilderness where he purifies our hearts. Let's take up our armor when he calls us forth into new territory. He is the one who goes before us, and he is the one who is with us. What a wonderful God! What a wonderful Savior!

Emmanuel, you are God with us. Thank you for the power of your presence in my life. Give me eyes to see the areas where you are already fighting for my freedom. You are wonderful!

DON'T STOP

"But don't stop! Pursue your enemies!
Cut off their retreat and don't let them reach their cities,
for Yahweh your God has given them into your hand!"

JOSHUA 10:19

*L*et us not grow complacent about the call of God on our lives when things seem to be under control and calm. Let us be as bold as lions, continuing to move forward in the courage of his presence and his promises. When we stop short of the fullness that he offers, it is we who suffer for it, not God.

There will be times to rest, and there will be times to push forward. Let us encourage one another in faith to keep going when we see that there is more breakthrough just ahead. Let us be people of perseverance, knowing that follow-through is as important as our intentions. Let us heed the wisdom of the God-lovers around us, and let's keep moving forward in the grace-strength of the Spirit when there is more ground to take in faith.

Powerful Lord, I rely on your Spirit to fuel my passion and purpose. When I grow weary but there is more left to pursue, encourage me through others and through your presence. I don't want to stop too soon when there is more victory waiting.

COURAGEOUS CONQUERORS

Joshua said to his officers, "Never be afraid of your enemies
or let them discourage you. Be strong and filled with courage!"

JOSHUA 10:25

*T*he faithfulness of God is our source of strength and courage. He moves in powerful and merciful ways to give us the fullness of his life. Christ in us is the hope of glory; his life is already ours through fellowship with his Spirit.

Why should we fear the unknowns ahead? Why would we doubt the overpowering love of God that covers all of our sin and shame? Jesus is our liberator, and he leads us into his victory over death. His life within us empowers us to be the courageous conquerors that he has called us to be. It is his mercy at work in our lives that makes a way where we could see none. Let's trust him when we feel discouragement knocking on the door of our hearts. He is overwhelmingly good, and darkness flees in the light of his presence.

Great God, you are my courage, and you are my strength. With eyes fixed on you, I will not be discouraged when lies try to tear me down. I stand on the truth of your love and of your abundant mercy.

ALL-POWERFUL GOD

By the power of Yahweh, the city and its king
were handed over to the Israelites.

JOSHUA 10:30

Where have you seen the power of Yahweh at work in your life?
Have there been unexpected turns of favor that you could not
explain? There is no detail too small that God does not consider.
He loves to work on behalf of his people, moving in both large
and little ways. Everything he does is with the thread of his mercy
running through it.

We are each part of a larger whole. Our lives intertwine into a
greater tapestry than we can perceive. Are we convinced, as Paul
said in Romans, that every detail of our lives is continually woven
together for good? It is not simply for our own good but also for
the good of our families, communities, and churches. May we look
from the higher perspective of Jesus, where he invites us to see
how he is moving in our lives and in the earth.

*Powerful One, give me your perspective today. I long to look from
the vantage point of eternity, where you see all things clearly.
Thank you for what you are doing.*

SECRETS OF CONQUEST

Yahweh empowered Joshua to conquer the whole region, including the hill country, the southern desert, the western foothills, and the mountain slopes.

JOSHUA 10:40

*W*hat are the great secrets of conquest hidden in the history of Israel? It is simpler and clearer than we may have anticipated. It is the relationship of God with Joshua, and therefore Israel, that led to victory after victory. Joshua did not depend on his own understanding but on Yahweh's instruction. It was not his own strength that led Israel into battle but the Spirit of God that empowered him.

As we lean into the tangible presence of God with us here and now, we will find the strength and power to move in obedience to his Word. We have been given unhindered access to God through Jesus, and there is nothing that keeps us from him. Let's humble ourselves in his presence, seek his face before we move in action, and rely on his grace to empower us. He is all that we need to overcome the difficulties in this life. He is our great strength and our even greater hope.

Lord, I look to you today. I look to you every day. Speak to me, whisper your words of life, and strengthen me with your truth. I need you more than I need anything else.

OUTNUMBERED

They came out in full force with a multitude of horses
and chariots. Their vast armies were as numerous
as the grains of sand on the seashore.

JOSHUA 11:4

*H*ave you ever been overwhelmed by your circumstances? Perhaps you faced a problem that looked like there was no chance for you to come out on the other side still intact. No matter how outnumbered you may feel, no matter the odds against you, God has not abandoned you. He has not left you to figure out your way on your own.

When God declares our victory, we can take courage in his help. He does not lead us into destruction but into triumph. He is the one who fights for us as we go into battle. The Commander of Angel Armies is the one who goes before us. May we fix our eyes on Jesus and keep them there! Let's let him handle the overwhelming worries we cannot control, and let's partner with his purposes as we move where he guides us. He is trustworthy, he is faithful, and he is victorious.

Sovereign Lord, I follow where you lead. I shift my gaze from the overwhelming odds stacked against me and fix my eyes on you. I trust you.

SPIRITUAL BATTLES

Joshua waged war with all those kings over a long period.

JOSHUA 11:18

Some spiritual battles we cannot easily win, and we cannot quickly overcome. Thankfully, God will ultimately make us victorious in all things as we submit our lives to him. When the battles last longer than we expect, let us not become discouraged. God does not promise quick fixes or shortcuts for all of our problems. He does promise to be with us in them and to give us victory.

If there is a battle that you have grown weary in fighting, lean into the presence of God today. As you make room for him, he will pour his plentiful peace into your heart. As he speaks his love over you, he will calm the chaos of your doubts. He is not defeated, and neither are you. Let him love you to life in the pools of his presence. He gives refreshing rains when we are bone-dry. He leads us to rest when we are weary. Take heart and take hope in him, for he is for you. He will never abandon you.

Redeemer, lead me into the peace of your presence and strengthen me in my innermost being. I long to commune with you and be refreshed in your love. Empower me, give me endurance, and lift my heaviness today.

LEGACY

Moses and the Israelites conquered the two kings,
Sihon and Og. Moses, the servant of Yahweh,
divided their land east of the Jordan among the tribes of Reuben,
Gad, and half the tribe of Manasseh.

JOSHUA 12:6

*B*efore Joshua and the Israelites crossed over the Jordan into the promised land, there were battles already fought and won under Moses' leadership. The legacy of those victories was the assignment of those conquered lands to certain tribes. Israel had already fought and won part of their inheritance before they expanded into new territory.

Perhaps you find yourself in a new season of life, needing to trust God in new ways. It may feel intense and new now, but once you have traveled through a bit, you will see how faithfully God works in and through your life. As you look back on previous battles and trials that felt impossible at the time may you draw fresh courage from having lived through them. Where can you see the thread of God's mercy through your life? What legacy have you already built your life upon?

Faithful One, thank you for the clarity you offer when I look back on past experiences through the lens of hindsight. Show me my legacy and give me courage to keep moving forward in strength and faith.

FIGHT FOR YOUR INHERITANCE

On the west side of the Jordan, Joshua and the Israelites defeated
thirty-one kings, from Baal-Gad in the Lebanon Valley in the north
to Mount Halak in the south near Edom.

JOSHUA 12:7

When God calls us to move ahead in his strength and take
territory that he has promised us, it will not be by a snapping of
the fingers or wishful thinking. Territory is taken by force. What
do you need to fight for? What is it that requires your courageous
movement forward? Where is God leading you to battle for your
freedom? What has he already declared as yours?

May you find the grace-strength of God in his presence with you
today. Ask him for what you need. Is it vision you are lacking?
Ask him for fresh perspective. Is it clarity for which way to turn?
Ask him for his wisdom. He does not withhold anything that you
require. He is all-powerful, and he will help you overcome anything
that threatens to overtake you. Remember, he does not barter
in fear or shame. Let his love propel you into the places he has
prepared for you to go.

*Jesus, give me strength in your presence. Fill me with courage
to conquer every battle I face. I depend on you, not on my own
strength. Thank you!*

PERMANENT PORTION

Then Joshua divided this land among the tribes of Israel
and gave them their portions as permanent possessions.

JOSHUA 12:7

*O*ur kingdom inheritance is a *permanent portion*. By grace, we
have been saved through faith. When we yield our lives to Jesus,
following him on the path of surrendered love, we are walking into
the inheritance of his kingdom. There is peace for those who put
their trust in God. There is restoration and redemption.

Israel had to partner with Yahweh through obedience in order to
receive their inheritance. So it is with us. As we partner with God
by following his kingdom will and ways, we enter into the fullness
of our inheritance. There, what we receive is our permanent
possession. Let's look at the fruit of God's kingdom and his
promises for those who yield their lives to him. There is so much
more available to us than what we have yet claimed through faith.

*Yahweh, thank you that your salvation is strong and sure. I look
to you for the fullness of the promises you have made, and I align
my life with what you say. I receive all that you have to offer; I am
yours! Thank you.*

KEEP RECORD

Here is the list of the thirty-one kings destroyed by Joshua.

JOSHUA 12:9

*H*ave you ever read through a genealogy and wondered at its significance? Perhaps you marveled at the number of specifics you found in a recorded account. Through the details of history, we preserve what is true. We learn from our yesterdays when we take the lessons they present us and apply them today. The past can be our great teacher, and it can be the encouragement we need in the moment and for our future.

When we keep record of our own lives, we leave a smaller risk for the rewriting of history through rose-colored glasses. We do not remember things perfectly. We can also preserve the victorious moments we may have otherwise forgotten. There is power in the details of our stories. Take time to write down the prayers you pray and the answers you see, as well as the meaningful moments you don't want to forget. It will be a gift to you in the future.

Great God, thank you for moving so faithfully through my life. As I remember what you have done, and as I record what you are doing, I take encouragement from your loyal love. I open my heart, as well, to the lessons from my disappointments. How great you are!

THERE IS MORE

Yahweh spoke to him:
"Although you have reached a ripe old age,
a great deal of land remains for you to conquer."

JOSHUA 13:1

Joshua had been following the Lord for many decades when God spoke to him in this passage. Though he had led the Israelites into their promised land, Yahweh spoke to him regarding what lay ahead. There was still more territory to conquer. There was more blessing to lay hold of.

In the same way, we are complete in Christ. We have entered the promised land of his salvation that is sure and immovable. And yet, there is more spiritual territory for us to conquer. There is more blessing to possess. As we follow God, he will remind us that we have not reached the end of his goodness. We have not reached the pinnacle of our lives, no matter how old we are. There is always more to experience, always more to reach for in his abundant kingdom. May we keep moving ahead in him, for his love is never stagnant.

Good Father, thank you that there is so much more available in your kingdom that I have yet experienced. I want to know the all-surpassing goodness of your expansive love. As I move in you, move in my life.

TAKE HOLD OF WHAT GOD OFFERS

"The territory waiting for you to possess includes
all the land of the Geshurites and the Philistines."

JOSHUA 13:2

*H*ow wonderful it is that God speaks to us. How glorious it is that he leads us in his wisdom. When he has more for us to move into, he reveals it. In our movement toward him, he moves us into the new places he has prepared for us. There's no need to worry about getting it wrong when we live as those who passionately pursue God's presence. He reveals himself to those who look for him. He speaks to those who listen for his voice.

What territory is waiting for you? In what areas is God calling you to move forward in faith and courage? Where is he leading you with the confidence of his faithfulness? You are a partner and friend with the King of kings and Lord of lords. Do not hesitate to look to him for answers. He has all the strategies that you need. Rest in his steadfast love and move ahead as he leads you.

Good Shepherd, thank you for leading me in your love. I long to know you more and to hear the words you speak. I'm so grateful to know you and be known by you. I take hold of what you offer.

MOVING FORWARD

*"As the people of Israel advance,
I myself will drive out these peoples from before you!"*

JOSHUA 13:6

God is incredibly gracious with us. Even when he calls us to move forward in faith, we are not left to our own strength and capabilities. He goes before us, driving out the opposition we face. He clears pathways of peace. He moves in marvelous ways. He is our wonderful leader. He is our ultimate warrior-chief.

When the Lord calls you in a direction that requires courage, know that he makes a way for you. He never leads where he has not already gone. May your heart fill with resolution and confidence as his presence propels you. Don't hesitate at the borders of your comfort zone when he is offering you more as you step into the great unknown. Follow his lead, and you will find that he clears the path before you and offers you all the tools you need along the way. He is trustworthy.

All-powerful One, I trust you to do what I cannot and to lead me in the confidence of your strong love. You are my hope, and you are my vision. I look to you, and I follow you.

TRIBAL INHERITANCE

"Divide the land among the tribes of Israel
exactly as I have commanded you."

JOSHUA 13:6

*I*t is important that we know the Lord does not simply deal with us on an individual level. He has set us in families, in tribes, in communities, and in nations. May we know the power of his favor in relationship with others and not simply depend on our own isolated experiences.

There is so much power in community. We thrive together, and we grieve together. We lift each other up, and we could also tear each other down. Let us be mindful of how we interact with those we live, work, and journey with. We have been welcomed into the family of God, and it is interconnected and united in his love. There may be different tribes on this earth, but all tribes are united in Christ. May we learn from each other, depend on one another, and, above all, love one another well.

Jesus, you are the head over all. Under you, we are unified. Move my heart in love and connectedness with others when I would rather isolate. Teach me what true communion looks like in your family.

MOVE IN

"Divide among the other nine tribes and the other
half-tribe of Manasseh the territory west of the Jordan
to possess as their inheritance."

JOSHUA 13:7

Relationship with the Lord is not passive. What God offers we must take hold of. Imagine a father offering his child a beautifully wrapped present. He says to the child, "Here, I got this for you!" Now imagine that the child simply thanks the father but never unwraps the gift. What use is the gift to the child unless he opens it?

How often does God offer us something and we simply say "thanks" and then move on without actively receiving it? Are there gifts that you have neglected? Take some time with the Lord today and ask him to remind you of any gifts that he has offered that you have not yet opened. Some will take simple steps of faith, and others will take actively moving toward them to locate and possess. The Father's heart is always for you to know his love more, so let shame's voice quiet in his presence as you move closer to his purposes.

Father, thank you for the gift of your nearness. In your presence, remind me of gifts that I've forgotten about. I long to know you more and to walk in the fullness of your kingdom.

SHARE IN GOD'S OFFERING

Moses did not assign any land as an inheritance to the tribe of Levi, for their inheritance was to share in the sacrificial offerings made to Yahweh.

JOSHUA 13:14

The tribe of Levi was the priestly tribe of Israel. They were the ones who presided over the temple as priests and musicians. They served as guards of the temple or priests who offered sacrifices to the Lord on behalf of the people. They were servants of the Lord and his presence, for they presided over the temple where the ark of the covenant was kept.

As servants of God, they shared in the sacrificial offerings made to Yahweh. His provision was their provision. It is important that we recognize the responsibility of God's people to support those who have dedicated their lives to serving God and to the body of Christ. When we make offerings to the Lord, may we not neglect the portion of that offering that should go to those who serve God with their livelihoods. We get to take part in the priestly blessing of Levi through our own offerings today.

Yahweh, bless your people through the offerings I give you. I will not neglect blessing those who serve you through my own sacrifices. Thank you for your provision for all who look to you.

FULLNESS IN YAHWEH

Moses...said to them, "Yahweh, the God of Israel,
is to be your inheritance."

JOSHUA 13:33

When we live for God, it is not just his blessing that we have. He is our inheritance. The fullness of God is our sustenance, our provision, and our exceedingly abundant reward. What an amazing and humbling reality. Whatever we need, God has offered us in himself. Christ, the hope of glory, is our inheritance.

When you find yourself worried about how you will meet a need that you are ill-equipped to satisfy, look to Jesus. Let trust in his faithfulness be your guide into the peace of his presence. He will not fail you, and he will not leave you destitute. He has all the wisdom you need, every strategy you could ever imagine, and the provision you require. Trust him, for he is your faithful God. He is loyal in mercy, and he is your plentiful portion in every season of the soul.

Yahweh, I trust you to fulfill your promises and to be my abundant portion. Fill me with the clarity of your presence as I press into you today. I stand upon your unfailing Word that you are my inheritance.

REMEMBER WHAT HE HAS SPOKEN

Caleb said to Joshua, "Remember what Yahweh said to Moses about you and me while we were still at Kadesh Barnea."

JOSHUA 14:6

*E*very word that God speaks is full of purpose and power. He does not forget a single promise he has made. May we hold God to his word, for he is faithful. Let's remember what he has spoken to us. Let's recall what has been prophesied over us. He is our good and faithful Father, and he has not changed his mind.

The promises of God, as Paul says in Corinthians, find their "yes" and "amen" in him. Their fulfillment depends on his faithfulness. When we remember what he has spoken, we can build our own confidence on his steadfast character. We can present our case to God, knowing that when we speak his promises back to him, he is moved to act on it. He is not finished working out his plans and purposes in this earth, and he is not finished faithfully fulfilling his Word in our lives.

God, I carry your promises in my heart. I trust you to fulfill them as I walk in your ways. I am encouraged by your presence, and I am emboldened by your faithfulness. I will not stop remembering what you have said.

FAITHFUL OBEDIENCE

"I have been faithful and obedient to Yahweh, my God."

JOSHUA 14:8

*H*ow devoted are we to Jesus? How faithful are we to his Word? How much do we trust his heart? It is his kindness that leads us to repentance. It is his strong love that sets us free to walk in the ways of his kingdom. We love because he first loved us. We follow him because he is the way, the truth, and the life.

We honor Jesus with our lives when we live like he instructed. This is not to say that we need to be perfect. None of us can perfectly live according to his law. Jesus came to set the record straight, to show us the way to the Father, and to remove everything that hinders love in our lives. There is restoration, there is redemption, there is freedom in our Savior. How could we not give him our lives when he has not withheld even his own blood for us?

Jesus, I choose to follow you. Your love has set me free, and you consistently move in goodness. Your mercy is big enough for me and all my mistakes. It's large enough to cover the sins of the whole world. Thank you!

PLEAD YOUR CASE

"So here I am. It's been forty-five years since Yahweh made this
promise to Moses, when Israel journeyed through the wilderness."

JOSHUA 14:10

God invites us to show up completely as we are. Do we have a
case to make for God's promises? Let's not hesitate before him.
Is there a question we have to pose? We can ask it freely. Caleb
remembered the promise that Yahweh had made to him when
he was a younger man. As time went by, he never forgot it. He
discerned the time to plead his case before Joshua and before
Yahweh.

Caleb didn't present his case before they had crossed over into the
promised land. He offered it when there was already movement in
Israel claiming their promised territory. He took advantage of the
momentum that was already happening to ask for the blessing. He
did not go out on his own and try to take hold of what had been
promised either. He went first to Israel's leader for the blessing to
take hold of his promise. May we also discern the times we are in
and present our case before God and before others.

*God, here I am. With all that's on my heart and mind. I ask for
your wisdom and your blessing as I pour my thoughts out to you.*

CLAIM YOUR PROMISE

"Now give me the hill country that Yahweh promised me on
that day...I know that with the power of Yahweh helping me,
I will drive them out, just as Yahweh said!"

JOSHUA 14:12

Sometimes when we present our case before others, it is with
a gentle invitation. Other times, it is with confident assurance in
what we know is already ours. At these times, it is an opportunity
for others to join us in our own victory. May we be like farmers
who sense the changing of seasons and make movements to ready
the land for its use.

Is there a promise that has been guiding you? Is there a claim
you have staked on Jesus? These are no small matters. These are
building blocks of a life. They are foundational to our dreams.
These are our inheritance. Caleb didn't hesitate to claim the
promise that Yahweh had made him. He reminded Joshua of
what he himself had heard through Moses. This was a moment of
reckoning and assertion on the foundation of God's vow—his very
word. May we be as bold and insistent as Caleb.

*Lord, I will not shrink back or wait around when the winds of
change move me in the direction of my destiny. I will rise up with
boldness and push forward in the confidence of your name.*

BLESSED TO RECEIVE

Joshua spoke God's blessing over Caleb son of Jephunneh
and gave him Hebron as his inheritance.

JOSHUA 14:13

Joshua spoke the Lord's blessing over Caleb to conquer the
territory he was promised. He was blessed to receive the promise.
But that was not all. Caleb had to go into the land where there
were rumored giants to claim his inheritance. He needed to fight
for his promised legacy.

Caleb was full of courage. He knew that with God on his side, he
would be victorious. Yahweh had promised him that land, and
he believed that he would help him claim it as his own. When
we are blessed to receive our own promises, may we remember
that a conflict usually follows. May we not be surprised when this
happens. We march with the confidence of Yahweh going before
us and with us into our battles. We actively receive the inheritance
of his kingdom as we pursue the territory he has offered us.

*Great God, thank you for going with me into my battles. Thank
you for the promise of your favor and your help. No matter what
obstacles I face, I will not be afraid, for you are with me.*

No Inheritance Forgotten

> But he did have five daughters...They came before the priest Eleazar and Joshua son of Nun and the leaders, and said, "Yahweh commanded Moses to give us an inheritance among our relatives." So...he gave an inheritance to them.
>
> Joshua 17:3–4

When we read through the chronicles of history, we do not often encounter instances of daughters receiving the same inheritance as their male counterparts. The five daughters of Zelophehad, who were his only descendants, came before the priest Eleazar and Joshua, as well as the other leaders over Israel, and advocated for their inheritance. They reminded the leaders of Yahweh's command to Moses that they would have their own share.

In response, Joshua assigned them land in the same way and measure that he did their uncles. What a wonderful picture this is that no inheritance is forgotten. This was against the custom of the time, but Yahweh's Word always wins over customary practices. This is still true today. Where God has promised us an inheritance, we can count on his Word, no matter society's standard.

Yahweh, you are the one who gives, and you are the authority by which it is given. I will advocate for your Word and not my own way.

CLEAR GROUND

"If the hill country of Ephraim is too small for the large number of people in your tribes, then go into the forests... and clear ground for yourselves there."

JOSHUA 17:15

When our lives expand, sometimes we need to clear ground to make space. When we are already living in the fulfillment of our calling, instead of pushing further outward, let's look for where we can make room where our feet are already planted. We can become a bustling and successful city if we will use the land we have wisely.

Have you felt at a loss for how you could keep growing without moving into new areas? Have you sought God for answers and not had any direction? Look at the resources you already have at your disposal. Are there areas that can still be developed? Instead of overly focusing on the outward motion, let's take a look inward to develop what we already possess.

Wise One, give me clarity of vision to see where I can both clear ground and utilize the resources I already have at my disposal. Thank you for your wisdom and leadership. Thank you for the blessing of abundance!

EMPOWERED TO DO GREATER THINGS

"Therefore, I will give you the country as well. It is a forest, but Yahweh will empower you to take possession of it and clear it from one end to the other."

JOSHUA 17:18

The tribes of Ephraim and Manasseh were growing in number and outgrowing the shares of land that they were given. They approached Joshua to ask for more territory. In response, he instructed them first to clear the forests within their reach. He ensured them that Yahweh would empower them to clear the land and overcome the powerful Canaanites who lived in the plains.

When we ask for greater things, God will also often require us to courageously conquer and clear new territory. There is partnership in taking hold of the promise of God. He vows to empower us to overcome the obstacles in front of us. He promises to be with us in it, to strengthen us, and to fight on our behalf. We can confidently do the greater things with his emboldening presence.

Spirit of God, you are my source, my strength, and my supply. I rely on you! Fill me with your presence to walk with courage and obedience to your Word. Thank you for your strong help as I partner with you.

ISRAEL'S FIRST CAPITAL

After the Israelites had conquered the land,
all of them gathered at Shiloh,
and the priests set up the tabernacle.

JOSHUA 18:1

The Israelites moved the tabernacle of God's presence from the wilderness after seven years of conquest. Shiloh became the center of worship for several hundred years. In this place, Hannah later prayed to have a son and then dedicated her miracle answer, Samuel, to God. Shiloh was the first capital of Israel, the epicenter of Yahweh's presence.

Jesus is our Shiloh. When we focus our lives on Jesus Christ, he becomes our governmental center. He is the fullness of God, and we come to the Father through him. It is to him that we bring every problem, every quarrel, and every question. He offers us the wisdom, the direction, and the settlement that we seek. May we align our lives with his government, for he is our King.

King Jesus, you are the one I center my whole life around. It is your wisdom I seek, and it is your favor I long for. Thank you for accepting me into your kingdom and for guiding me into your ways.

FROM PASSIVITY TO PASSION

Joshua addressed the seven tribes...who had not yet received their inheritance: "How much more time will you waste until you go out and possess the land that Yahweh, the God of your ancestors, has given you?"

JOSHUA 18:2–3

Sometimes the promises we are waiting on in life are not delayed because of God but because of us. When we sit back and don't participate when God has already given clear directives, we are the ones deferring our hopes. Perhaps the areas we have grown passive in are the very areas that God is waiting for us to passionately pursue.

May this meet you where you are, not heaping shame on your present season, but empowering you to know what is yours to do and what is yours to claim. Are there areas where you once felt hopeful but where now you feel indifferent? Is there something you have known you needed to do but have avoided doing? May today be the day you throw off excuses and lean into God's empowering presence for renewed desire, courage, and strength.

Yahweh, thank you for the reminder of my part in our partnership. I take you at your word, and I choose to lay aside my excuses for inaction. Help me, Jesus, to be courageous and walk forward in faith.

DOING YOUR PART

"So let each of the seven remaining tribes select three men
and send them to me. I will send them out to survey
and make a map of the entire land."

JOSHUA 18:4–7

*W*hat a wondrous, gracious God we serve. He gives more
chances than we deserve. He consistently pursues the best for us
even when we don't know how to do it for ourselves. His wisdom
is unrivaled and his grace is like an ocean.

As we mature in our faith, we find that our young understanding
transforms with experience and with greater responsibility.
Maturity knows that we have agency in our own dreams. We
have choices to make, and we have paths to walk. We have work
to do. We are not children who rely on the milk of our mothers
any longer. We are grown men and women, partnering with the
purposes of God with our lives. Let's remember that as we grow,
God continues to lead and guide us, but it may look different than
it did at first, when we were young and helpless in our faith.

*Lord, I'm so grateful to partner with you in life, in pursuits, and in
healing. I not only depend on you, but I also put in the work that
is mine to do.*

DETAILED DESCRIPTION

"Go through all the land and write down its description.
When you bring the description back here to me,
I will ask Yahweh in Shiloh to divide the land among your tribes."

JOSHUA 18:8–9

*G*od is alive in the details of our lives. He is active in the particulars of our stories. Do we have a vague idea about where we are headed, or do we have clear vision of what we are moving toward in life? What are the details of the promised land we are moving into? It is important to know what our hopes are and what the realities are.

Take some time with the Lord to write down the description of what you are moving toward. What is it that he has said? What is required of you? What will it take to get there? What are the important elements that will be there when you arrive? Proverbs says that we make plans for our futures within our hearts, and the Lord chooses the steps we take to get there. It is a partnership.

Lord, thank you for the privilege of partnering with you. I see the purpose in looking at the details of your promises and moving forward toward them. Lead me with your love.

GOD'S CHOICE

> Then Joshua cast lots in Yahweh's presence at Shiloh and assigned a section of the land to each of the remaining tribes of Israel.
>
> JOSHUA 18:10

There are no winners and losers in the kingdom of our Redeemer. We all are blessed to receive what he portions out to us. No matter what our land looks like, we all have access to the same abundance of his resources. There is more than enough peace, joy, love, patience, power, and help, as well as so much more in his presence.

Have you ever looked at another's life and wished for their home, their land, their family, or something else? We miss out on the treasures in our own lives if we get caught up in the trap of comparison. God has not offered you a lesser inheritance. There is abundance available to you in the fulfillment of his promises toward you. The gifts he offers you are specifically tailored to your life. May you find joy, peace, and fulfillment in the places where he has given you domain and authority.

Provider, I trust that what you offer me is good. In fact, I trust that it is abundantly better than I have realized. Thank you for the inheritance I have in your kingdom.

April

WARRIOR-CHIEF

All the people of Israel gathered in front of the tabernacle...
When they finished dividing the land into its regions, the Israelites
gave their warrior-chief, Joshua son of Nun, his inheritance.

JOSHUA 19:49–51

The act of the nation of Israel giving their leader, Joshua, his own inheritance is a beautiful picture of how we bless Jesus with what we have been given. How can we honor our great warrior-chief with our lives? What can we offer him from our own inheritance in him?

Though Joshua was simply a man, he was the divinely appointed leader over Israel. The people knew this. We can learn something from his leadership here. He was a servant leader, just as Jesus was. He did what Yahweh told him to do, and he did not use his leadership for his own gain. He did not use his authority to give himself an inheritance, but he let the people decide after they had all been given their own. May we lead in humility and in obedience to God's Word, doing what God tells us to do. And may we honor those who have led us in integrity, just as Jesus leads us in truth.

Lord, thank you for your example of servant-leadership. I humble myself in your love and follow your lead. My life is yours.

CITIES OF ASYLUM

Yahweh instructed Joshua: "A person who accidentally...
kills someone will need a place of asylum—
a city where he can run for safety."

JOSHUA 20:1–3

*G*od knows our propensity for blame and revenge. His ways are much better than our ways though. He knows our hearts, knows our intent, and he has made provision for us to find refuge in his love. As followers of Jesus, we should also be safe spaces where the innocent can find shelter.

What would life be like if every accidental injury or offense were returned in kind? There would certainly be chaos and at the very least a heightened need to be on one's guard. Thankfully, God has provided us a place of refuge in his presence. He is our just judge and our defense. We can find safety in him at all times. Let's not hesitate to run to find sanctuary in him when others refuse to hear our case. Let's run to him, for he hears the cries of our hearts, and he knows the intent of our actions.

Yahweh, thank you for providing shelter for your people. Your ways are so much better than the ways of this world. I run into the safety of your presence, where my heart finds rest.

Explain Your Case

"The one...shall escape for protection to one of these cities
and stand at the entrance to the city gates and explain his case
to the leaders of the city."

JOSHUA 20:4–5

*H*as there ever been a time when you have felt completely disregarded and unheard? Perhaps someone has made up their mind about you without getting to know you first. Maybe you hurt someone unintentionally but were not given the opportunity to explain yourself. When we feel unheard, unseen, and misrepresented, we may struggle to trust those around us.

God is full of truth, full of clarity, and he is completely unbiased. He sees things as they are, and he knows the heart of every human. He knows our motivations and our leanings. He understands our intentions and still calls us to walk on the path of his humble love. May we find respite and relief in his presence today, knowing that we are completely seen, known, and understood. State your case to him, for he is always listening.

Lord, thank you for seeing me, knowing me, and understanding me. Thank you for being a safe shelter where I can say anything. Even as I open up to you, instruct me with your incomparable wisdom.

THE INNOCENT PROTECTED

"When the one looking for revenge comes after him,
the leaders of the city must protect him and not hand him over,
for he killed the person accidentally and without premeditation."

JOSHUA 20:5

In his Sermon on the Hillside in Matthew 5, Jesus said that our lives are like shining beacons of light. We are like a city on a hill that is easily seen from a far distance. Are we safe places for the vulnerable to take shelter? Are we welcoming of the foreigner, the traveler, and the falsely accused? Are we defenders of the weak?

When we let our light shine before others, we reflect the light of God. What does it mean to shine our light? Is it not to walk in the way of love, as Jesus directed us? He has shown us the way to go, the way to live, and the way to exemplify his kingdom patterns in this world. Let's welcome those looking for refuge and relief. Let's be a place of peace for the tormented. Is that not what Christ is for us?

Savior, I am so grateful for your refuge. I want to be a safe place for others. Teach me, mold me, and make me bold in your love.

REMAIN

"He must remain in the city until he has had a public trial;
then he must remain protected in the city."

JOSHUA 20:6

Jesus is our place of refuge. We can take shelter in him at all times, for we have been united with him through his Spirit. There is not a moment where we are without his love, and his very presence resides within us. With yielded hearts and surrendered lives, we dwell in the safety of his care.

Let us remain in him. There is no reason to wander outside the walls of his fellowship. We have been brought in by the blood of the Lamb, and we remain under his watchful care. He does not turn us away, and our great High Priest will never leave us. He is our constant covering. Let us linger in his presence, as a branch flourishes as it remains in the vine. He is our life-source, our strength, and our strong defense. As we remain in him, our lives will bloom with his Spirit fruit.

Jesus Christ, you are my safe place. I remain in your love, even as your love surrounds me. May I always be found here in the safety of your watchful care. Your presence is my greatest peace.

HEAVENLY REFUGE

These were the designated cities of refuge.
Any Israelite or any foreigner living among them...
could run to one of these cities for protection.

JOSHUA 20:9

The kingdom of God is not located in cities founded by men. It is greater than the kingdoms that rise and fall throughout human history. It is far loftier than any fortress could contain. If the earth is God's footstool, how great, then, is the city where he dwells?

One day, we will see clearly, but for now we have only glimpses of God's glorious ruling realm. When Jesus returns to rule and reign, he will usher in the fullness of his kingdom by restoring the earth. Until then, we trust in his unfailing love to lead us by faith. By the fruit of his Spirit, we know what his presence promotes. He is full of peace, full of joy, full of hope, full of love, always bringing light to the shadows and life to what decays. He is our heavenly refuge, and he always will be.

King Jesus, I long for the day when I will see you face-to-face. You are my holy hope and my heavenly hiding place. Give me a glimpse of your greater glory today.

No More Guilt

He could live there safely until he had a fair trial,
and unless he had been proven guilty,
he could not be killed by the one seeking revenge.

JOSHUA 20:9

In Jesus, we are sheltered by his mercy-offering. The blood of his covenant has completely covered our shame and our guilt. He is our righteousness, and he is the one who purifies us from all of our sins. There is nothing that the power of his blood cannot redeem.

The new covenant that Jesus made through his sacrifice removed the power of all that separated us from his love. His love overcame death itself, taking on our shame, our fear, and our guilt. We have been set free to rest in the safety of his saving grace. He is the city of refuge that we can run into to find shelter. Once there, we never need to leave. May we find our peace in him. He has broken down every barrier and become our reconciling peace.

Redeemer, thank you for removing my guilt with the power of your love. I remain in you, resting in your strong mercy. Fill me with a fresh portion of your peace today.

ASK AND YOU'LL RECEIVE

The ancestral heads of the Levites went to Eleazar the priest...
and said, "Yahweh instructed through Moses for you to give us
cities to live in and pasturelands around the cities for livestock."

JOSHUA 21:1–2

The biblical precedent for asking and receiving does not begin
or end with this example. Jesus told his followers, "Every persistent
one will get what he asks for [and] every persistent seeker will
discover what he longs for" (Matthew 7:8). Do we ask for what
God has promised us? Do we seek after what he has placed in our
hearts? Our longings point us to God, and they direct us to our
destinies in him.

May you have the boldness to ask the Lord for what he has already
promised you. Do not be discouraged when you see others
moving forward in life. Press in where you are and look straight at
Jesus. He is right there with you. He is the giver of all good things,
so take up your cause with him. He will not reject you. Remind
yourself of what he has said and ask him for it.

*Lord, thank you for the promises you have spoken over my life. I
won't compare my life with others today. I look to you, and I ask
you to fulfill what you have already offered.*

A BLESSING TO OTHERS

Yahweh had commanded through Moses to draw lots to see what cities the Levites would receive. So they drew lots, and the people of Israel gave them these cities together with the pasturelands around them.

JOSHUA 21:8

*G*od does not forget anyone—not a tribe, not a nation, not a single family. He has placed us in communities, and his offer of inheritance in his kingdom does not leave anyone out. We, as people of God, are conduits of his love. He is the ultimate provider, and yet we are called to reflect his image.

Are there those among us who have great need? Let's be the living expression of God's love by taking care of each other. Those of us who have much to give should consider that as we offer help to those with less, we are also making an offering to God. Generosity is a kingdom value. Sharing in each other's joys and sufferings, both emotionally as well as with our resources, is a way to live with surrendered love as our highest value. May our lives reflect the incomparable values of God's kingdom.

Merciful One, I want to live as your loving reflection. Help me to serve others quickly and freely and to be generous with what you have given me. It's all yours!

COSTLY GIFTS

The Levites received from the other tribes of Israel a total
of forty-eight cities, each with the pasturelands around them.

JOSHUA 21:41–42

The Levites received lands from the other tribes of Israel, just
as Yahweh had instructed. These were lands that the other tribes
fought for with their very lives. They did not try to back out of their
duty; they knew that they all had something to contribute to the
priestly tribe.

God still takes care of those who serve his tabernacle. Not all
are called to be priests or missionaries. Those who are called will
be covered by the covenant that God is provider. It is also our
responsibility, as those with resources that we have worked hard
for, to give a share to those who serve God as their vocation.
No matter how hard we have fought for our inheritance, it is not
wholly ours to keep to ourselves. May we be generous and wise in
our giving, not holding too tightly to our resources.

*Gracious God, I don't want to miss out on a single element or
value of your kingdom. I submit my resources to your leadership
and freely give without regret the portion you lead me to give.*

SETTLED IN THE PROMISE

Yahweh gave Israel all the land he had promised their ancestors.
They took possession of the land and settled there.

JOSHUA 21:43

God is faithful to fulfill his promises. The way we receive them may look different than how we may have expected, but his faithfulness is evident, nonetheless. Let us not miss out on what God is doing by being resistant to how it comes. Sometimes the gift will humble us in its generosity. Let's not resist it by being too proud. Other times, the one who offers it may give us pause. Again, let's not resist the promise because of the way it is offered.

We partner with the promises of God by taking hold of them when they are presented. We take possession of the gift, and we settle there. Are there any promises you have resisted taking possession of because you didn't love the way it was offered? Humble yourself before the Lord, ask him for his perspective, and take hold of what is yours. Settle in his peace and cultivate gratitude in the land you are given.

Faithful One, forgive me for where I have resisted what you have offered because of the one who offered it. I want to take hold of all that you have to offer. I humble myself before you now.

PROMISED LAND REST

Yahweh kept his promise and gave them peace in the land just as he had promised to their forefathers.

JOSHUA 21:44

*W*hen we have fought long, hard battles, what we long for is peace. Ask anyone from a war-torn place what their deepest longing was when they were in the midst of unrest. They may reflect that they longed for a sense of safety, to be able to rest in their homes without fear. They may insist that being able to live a normal life without the threat of violence was what they missed the most. Under, over, through it all, what they longed for was peace.

Jesus has offered us peace in his presence. It is not a fragile peace that could be upset at any moment. It is not like the treaties that nations make with one another. It is lasting peace, and it is ours through fellowship with him here and now. May we enter into the promise of his perfect peace as we turn to him today. He is ever so near and ever so ready to calm our fears with his lavish love.

Jesus, you are the peace that keeps me, even in the midst of my battles and storms. Fill me with your rest, as you promised you would. Thank you!

FAITHFUL AND TRUE

Yahweh didn't break a single promise that he made to the people of Israel. He faithfully kept every promise he made to them.

JOSHUA 21:45

The Lord doesn't forget a single word that he speaks. All that he once offered in the fullness of his love is still available. Stir up your own longings as you remember the promises of God over your life. Let them lead you to his throne room in prayer. Jesus is faithful and true, and he will not fail to meet you with the abundance of his revelatory mercy.

Just as Yahweh didn't break a single promise that he made to the people of Israel, he will not break a single promise that he has made to us. He will faithfully follow through on every single one. May we find our courage and confidence in his unchanging character, not in our own abilities to make things happen. He is so much more reliable than we could ever dream of becoming. And yet, the more time we spend with him, the more like him we become. What an amazing truth!

Unchanging One, thank you for being faithful in all that you do. I am undone in your presence; meet me with the overwhelming goodness of your grace as I look to you today.

HONORABLE MENTION

"You have done all that Moses the servant of Yahweh
commanded, and you have obeyed me in everything
I have commanded."

JOSHUA 22:2

Living a life of surrender to the Lord is honorable. It is not
without its challenges, but it is also not without its rewards. It is a
beautiful thing to encourage others when you recognize how they
are living with integrity, honor, and submission to God. To validate
another's dedication can build up their confidence and strengthen
them in their resolve.

How often do we take for granted those in our lives who show up
for us? May we take the time today to honor those who have been
faithful friends. May we recognize how others serve us well and
honor them for it. It could make all the difference for someone
who has felt unseen. Let's be those who call out the greatness in
each other and build each other up in grace, love, and strength.
Let's be generous with our praise and encouragement, just as God
is generous with his love and kindness toward us.

*Lord, thank you for putting people in my life who love well. As I
reach out in encouragement today, may others be built up in your
love through me.*

HELP TO THOSE IN NEED

"Through it all, you've never deserted your fellow Israelites
and were always there to help them."

JOSHUA 22:3

When times of trial and trouble come, it is the helpers who run
to the rescue. How do we help those in need? Are we a listening
ear to the hurting? Do we cover meals for those overwhelmed
with grief? Do we pay for groceries for those struggling to feed
their families? Pride has no place in the kingdom of God. We all
will have needs that we cannot meet at some point. May we give
freely and generously when we can, and may we not refuse help
when we need it.

There is tremendous strength in a community showing up for
those who are struggling. May we not live so isolated from the
needs of our neighbors that we build walls instead of opening our
homes. Every genuine gesture of kindness and help counts. May
we not diminish our small offerings, for the widow's mite is as
valuable as the gold of kings.

*Loving Lord, you are the best example of help I can find. I want
to look like you in generosity of heart, of resources, and of mind.
May I never hold back when I see another in need. Lead me in
your compassion.*

LEARN GOD'S COMMANDS

"Make sure you obey every command and instruction
Moses, Yahweh's servant, gave you."

JOSHUA 22:5

There is purpose in every instruction that God has given. May we look for the wisdom of his love through what was revealed in times before. The Word of God is full of stories of God's faithfulness. It is filled with examples of his mercy. It is made up of the power and glory of God meeting with humankind in our messes, as well as our triumphs.

When we look at the law through the lens of Jesus, we see what he was pointing at all along. The whole of the law can be summed up in loving God with our whole hearts, minds, and lives. When we love him, we also love those around us the way he loves—with their best interest at heart. His love is not shallow or easily upset. It is patient, kind, and gracious. It is not easily offended. Let's learn what God has already revealed through his Word and let it draw us to himself in the fellowship of his Spirit.

Yahweh, I believe that you are the one true God. As I submit my life to your ways, lead me into the abundant life-fruit of your kingdom.

WAYS OF GOD

"Love Yahweh! He is your God,
so walk in his ways and obey his commands!"

JOSHUA 22:5

*T*he ways of God are unlike our own human tendencies. Though we are prone to criticism, judgment, and revenge, God is long-suffering in love, endlessly hopeful, and full of mercy. Let's love him, not only with our hearts, but also with our very lives.

If we claim that Jesus is our God, then our lifestyles and choices must reflect this. If Jesus is our God, then we have no excuse for any lack of love toward another. The one who instructed us to love our enemies, to lay down our lives for our friends, and to submit ourselves to each other in love, has not changed his mind about how we should live. His law of love is extensive, applying to every relationship and circumstance we face. In him, we are called to act justly, to love mercifully, and to walk humbly with our God.

Gracious Lord, I lay down every excuse I have for my unwillingness to love others. I walk in your ways, humbling my heart before you. May I live with justice, mercy, and humility keeping me close to you.

Heart and Soul

"Cling to him and serve him diligently
with all your heart and with all your soul!"

JOSHUA 22:5

What does it mean that we should cling to God? Is it not the unrelenting turning of our attention to him throughout our day? Is it not the continual submission of our will to his own? He is faithful to help us. We do not need to perfectly walk in his ways, for surely we would fail. Let's cling to him, holding tightly to the love that already holds us close.

With our awareness set on God, our hearts expand in response. He gives, and we receive. He speaks, and we respond. He moves, and we are moved. With all our heart and soul, everything we have fixed on him, we get to serve him with our lives. He is the goodness we long for. He is the fullness of all that we strive to know in this life. We have been welcomed into the family of God through Jesus. We are dearly loved children. Every moment is an opportunity to know him more. May we give him access to our hearts whenever we think of it. He is so very near.

Spirit, I reach out for you, even as you surround me with your peace. I love you more than I can express.

SENT OUT WITH BLESSING

Joshua spoke a blessing over them
and sent them on their way, and they settled there.

JOSHUA 22:6

*W*hen we see others successfully moving toward their dreams, do we bless them? Let's get rid of every curse of jealousy that keeps us from cheering each other on in love. Where God moves and blesses, let us also add our blessing. We should never be threatened by another's success. God has an abundance of blessings for all of us, and though they may take different shapes, he is not stingy.

When we look with gratitude on what we have been given, even while holding on to the promises of God for what we have not yet received, we can celebrate with those who have conquered their fears and moved into new territory in their lives. Let us, with peace, joy, and love, bless others as we cling to hope. Another's victory is our encouragement. The Lord is good to all that he has made, so let us rejoice.

Faithful One, you are my hope and my life. May I live with love, blessing those who are moving into their destinies, even while I wait on you for my own.

GODLY GENEROSITY

"You are free to go. You leave for your homes rich—
with great herds of cattle, silver and gold...
Share with your friends and families everything you took
from your enemies."

JOSHUA 22:8

*W*hen we have fought hard to get to where we have arrived in life, the treasures we have collected along the way can feel like our just reward. Even in this, there is an opportunity to reflect the nature of God in how we view our abundance. The opposite is also true: we can become lovers of wealth and status more than lovers of God.

Joshua instructed the warriors to return to their homes and to share all that they had acquired with their friends and families. When we find ourselves with plenty, let's be generous in sharing with the people around us. Our own victory becomes the blessing of those we love. Let us not hoard what we have, but freely share it with those around us. There is tremendous blessing in sowing our wealth into our communities, but ivory towers don't benefit anyone.

Merciful One, thank you for your generosity toward your people. I long to reflect you in the generosity of my own life and resources. Help me to give the way that you do.

SELF-SERVING ALTARS

"We speak to you on behalf of all Yahweh's people.
Why did you rebel against Yahweh
and build this altar for yourselves?"

JOSHUA 22:16

An altar was used in the Old Testament as a sacred place for sacrifices and gifts offered to God. They were places specified to separate oneself, or one's nation or tribe, to God. There was only one altar in the temple in Shiloh, and it was the holy place where all of Israel offered their sacrifices to God. It was extremely significant and sacred.

Self-serving altars do not do us any good. They remove the acknowledgement of God's work in our lives. They instill a false sense of humility, for they are not the true altar of the Most High. Are we sacrificing our lives on the altar of God's mercy, or are we sacrificing our lives in the name of God but according to our own ideals? Let us humble ourselves before God and come to Jesus, the perfect and ultimate sacrifice. There is no other way to the Father but through him.

Jesus, I come to the altar where you lead me to the Father. I lay my life on yours, giving you all the glory for what you have done, are doing, and will do. I worship you!

REMEMBER WHAT CAME BEFORE

"Haven't we had enough trouble from the terrible sin
we committed at Peor? There a plague came upon us
even though we belong to Yahweh."

JOSHUA 22:17

*H*ave we learned from our mistakes? Surely, God is full of
mercy toward us, but we also cannot escape the consequences
of our actions. When we live connected to the presence of God,
submitted to his ways, and following the loving lead of Jesus, his
kindness will correct us.

Sometimes our memories fail us, and we get caught in cycles that
we cannot see our way out of. In those times, our close friends,
family, and mentors can lovingly remind us that we have been
there before. With their concern and counsel, we can choose to
redirect ourselves. Community is so important for our soul and
spiritual help—we need each other. Especially for the areas we fail
to see ourselves. May we be submitted to God and to one another
in love. With each other's help, we can see the bigger picture.

*Gracious One, thank you for the wisdom of fellowship with
others. Help me to be humble in your love and to receive
correction with an open heart, defenses down.*

REBELLION AFFECTS EVERYONE

"If you rebel against him today,
he will be angry with everyone in Israel tomorrow."

JOSHUA 22:18

*R*ebellion is not a small thing. It is an act against authority, and in the case of Israel, the unity of centralized worship to Yahweh. To oppose the unity of Israel was to break down the bond that held them together. Though this was not the intent of the tribes, it was no less a threat to the others who misinterpreted their motivation.

Can you recall someone in your life who rebelled against the unifying force of family or friends? How did their actions affect the rest of you? Undoubtedly, one person's revolt influences those who are closest to them. There are consequences to deal with. Grief at the rupture is inevitable. Perhaps addiction has lured someone away. May we have courage to graciously confront one another in love and work toward reconciliation and peace. God is full of redemption, wisdom, and love. May we reflect him well in our relationships.

Yahweh, I know that, in you, love unifies. There is no division in you. Help me to remain humble in your compassion and to be a promoter of peace in my relationships.

RETURN

"If you think your land is defiled,
then come back to Yahweh's land,
where his tabernacle stands at Shiloh."

JOSHUA 22:19

There is always an invitation to return to the land of our God. There, his mercy reigns and his kingdom ways rule. He is full of compassion to restore us, and he will not turn us away. Have we drifted into the land of self-serving fantasies that never fulfill? Have we forgotten our heavenly first love? Even if the answer to this is yes, we can choose this day whom we will live for.

May everything we do be lined with loyal love. As we stand for justice, may we also offer the kindness of mercy. As we fight for freedom for the oppressed, may we also stand in the hope of redemption. Love does not lead us astray, and it never will. Let's look at the fruit of our lives. Is peace our portion? Is patience evident? Is joy present? Is love apparent? If we recognize more destructive patterns in our lives, let us return today to the kingdom of our God and be restored in his loving-kindness. His power is more than enough to transform us.

Lord, I return to you today. Fill me with the power of your redemptive love, and purify my heart, mind, and soul in your presence.

HOLY WARNING

"Don't forget what happened to Achan! Yahweh told us,
'Destroy everything in the city of Jericho.' But Achan...
did not obey Yahweh's command regarding the devoted things."

JOSHUA 22:20

*L*earning from history is important to building our future.
We should not ignore the mistakes of past leaders, nations,
and people. They are tools for us; their destruction can be our
instruction. Let us not be unwise by ignoring the damaging
patterns of those who have gone before us. Let us use the wisdom
of lessons learned to refine and guide us in our own decisions.

Do we heed the concerned cries of others who call us to look
at historical precedents? Do we brush them off as unnecessary
worries because we do not see the connection? Let us not be
overrun by fear, but let's listen to those who may have insight that
we do not. Let's take seriously the warnings they present so that
we may sift the truth from lies and the reality from fears.

*Holy One, I do not want to have a hardened heart toward warning
and correction. May I discern, with wisdom and an open heart to
understand, the patterns I may be taking part in that don't reflect
your kingdom.*

MISUNDERSTOOD

"Yahweh is the God of all gods!
We appeal to God Almighty as our witness.
He knows why we did this, and we want you to know too!"

JOSHUA 22:22

There will be times when others misinterpret our motivations. They may be concerned and jump to conclusions without knowing where we are coming from. Misunderstandings are a part of life, for we are not perfect, and we don't discern everything correctly.

When someone confronts us with their ideas of what we are doing, how do we react? Do we shut down and pull away because of the offense we feel? No one is a mind reader. Communication is so important, and that is true in every relationship. When we are misunderstood and we value the relationship with the one who confronts us, let us enter into the discomfort of confrontation and explain ourselves. God knows our hearts, and he knows our motivations. What he does not judge, others may still not understand. When we have the opportunity, let's clear the air and let our true hearts be known with those who make space to listen.

God Almighty, I'm so grateful that you never misinterpret my motivations. Even so, help me to be open with my process and thinking with those who I care about when they question me.

WALK BY FAITH, NOT FEAR

"We love Yahweh! We were afraid that in the future your descendants will say to our descendants, 'Who are you?'...We did build an altar, but not for burning sacrifices or making offerings."

JOSHUA 22:24–26

If these tribes had consulted with the others before they went about building their altar, this whole misunderstanding could have been prevented. If they had not let fear drive their actions, the other tribes would have already known what they were doing.

The fear of man keeps us from thriving. It keeps us from fully trusting, both God and others. There are unnecessary conflicts that arise out of our playing small and making assumptions of others, rather than connecting with them in humility and honesty. When we feel the push of fear to rush us into action, may we slow down in the presence of God and ask ourselves what is motivating us. Haste leads to poverty, not only in our work ethics, but also in relationships. Let's work to stay connected in love, rather than disconnected in fear.

Spirit, bring to my attention when I am rushing in fear, rather than considering in love. Your love is peaceful, not frantic. Clothe me in the wisdom of faith as I walk in your ways.

VOW TO YAHWEH

"We built this altar to show to our people and to your people and to the generations to come that we will worship Yahweh at his tabernacle."

JOSHUA 22:27

We do not always know what inspires people to do what they do. Though it may look chaotic and unnecessary to us, it may feel deeply necessary to them. Instead of judging others for how they deal with their uncertainty, may we open our hearts in Christ's compassion, seeking to understand where they are coming from. In this expansive movement, we make space for their experience while also allowing for a difference in opinion.

We each devote our lives to God in unique ways. We don't do it perfectly, for we are only human, and our understanding and capacity are limited. God gives us grace for our expressions of faith, and so should we give the same consideration to others. Unity of purpose is not the same as uniformity. There is room for differing expressions of devotion. Let us not judge another's vow to God based on our own preferences.

Lord, I love that there is diversity in your kingdom and in creation. May I never judge what you don't. Help me to seek to understand others and to love them all the same, even when I don't agree with them.

SERVING THE SAME GOD

"Our descendants would reply: 'See the replica of the altar of Yahweh...made here at the border between us—not for burnt offerings or sacrifices, but as a witness that we both serve the same God.'"

JOSHUA 22:28

*T*here are symbols used to unite people outside of families and tribes. When you think about prominent Christian symbols, what comes to mind? You may think of the cross or the fish-like ichthus that the early church used. These are simply symbols, but they signal a kindred connection between members of the body of believers.

The family of God is larger than a nation, a language, or a specific people group. In Revelation, John described seeing an enormous multitude of people made up of "victorious ones" from every nation, tribe, people group, and language in the throne room of heaven (Revelation 7:9). We can expect if there will be representatives of each of these in the heavenly realm, then there are certainly as many diverse representatives on the earth. May we be people who reach past the differences that separate us to grab hold of what unites us under God.

Heavenly Father, thank you for the reminder that your kingdom is made up of people from every corner of the earth. May I see others through your lens and not my own.

PLACE OF HIS PRESENCE

"We would never build an altar to take the place of the altar which stands before his tabernacle, the place of his presence."

JOSHUA 22:29

*T*he place of God's presence is within the tabernacle. The altar sits in front of the temple of the Most High. But what does this mean to those of us who do not offer sacrifices at the altar of a physical temple? Where does God reside?

Paul illuminates this for us in his first letter to the Corinthians. He speaks of the body of believers, his united church, as the holy dwelling place of God on earth (1 Corinthians 3:16). He also says in that same letter that our individual bodies have become "the sacred temple of the Spirit of Holiness" (1 Corinthians 6:19). The Holy Spirit lives inside the sanctuary of our bodies, communicating Spirit to spirit—communing from deep to deep. So then, we know that whether together or on our own, the place of God's presence is with us through his Spirit. We are temples of the Living God.

Holy Spirit, make yourself at home within me. Mold me, teach me, and refine me with your healing presence. I am in awe of you and the power of your presence.

May

PEACE PROMOTED

The outcome pleased the Israelites and they praised God.
They spoke no more of going to war against the eastern tribes
to destroy the land where they had lived.

JOSHUA 22:33

*E*very peaceful resolution is a reason to praise God. When families are reconciled, cities are unified, and nations broker peaceful treaties, there is cause to rejoice. How have you experienced the relief and joy of peace after a time of tension? Perhaps it was in a relationship, or maybe it was in the tumultuous aftermath of a war. Hope keeps us open and searching for a space in which to connect and reconcile. When we do, there is a collective sigh of relief.

May we seek to be promoters of peace in the world and in our communities. Peace is not cheap, and it does not avoid the hard questions. It takes true listening to understand, and it moves forward toward mercy whenever possible. May we be those who do the hard work of confronting the harsh realities, while also keeping our hearts soft in hope and compassion.

Prince of Peace, I know that your peace is beyond any that the world gives. Their guarantees are empty, but yours are not. I choose to walk in your ways and pursue connection rather than combat.

WITNESS

The Reubenites and the Gadites called the altar Witness, for they said, "The altar stands as a witness to all that Yahweh is God."

JOSHUA 22:34

What "altars of witness" do you have in your life? Are there any miracles that you have experienced? Any provisions that God has made that have changed the trajectory of your life? Perhaps it was a fulfilled promise. Maybe it was the reconciliation of a relationship. It could have been a recovery from a sickness.

We all have these imprints of God's mercy in our lives. There are instances we cannot explain, favor that we cannot account for, and wonderful answers to prayers. Wherever there has been relief in your life, it is a reflection of God's kindness—of his endless goodness. May you recall the moments in your life that stand as altars of witness to the power of God and give him praise.

Faithful God, you are limitless in miraculous kindness. Your ways are beautiful, and your provisions do not miss a detail. Thank you for working in both small and big ways. Remind me of the wonders that you have done, as I look for the markers of your mercy throughout my life. You are so good!

Faith-Rest

Many years had passed since Yahweh had given Israel rest
from all their enemies, and Joshua was very old.

Joshua 23:1

*W*hen we find ourselves in peaceful seasons in life, let us
recognize the hand of God that has led us to rest. There are times
in life when we must march with courage and fight for our futures.
There are other times when God will fight for us, when we are in
the dark valleys of grief. Still at other times, there will be a sense
of peace, calm, and grounding. Let us not take for granted the
seasons of reaping the abundant harvest of peace.

Though many cultures in this world seem to elevate busyness,
there is also the other side of that coin that we must not forget:
rest. In order to work well and to move ahead, we must give
ourselves the time to refresh and rejuvenate. Wherever we find
ourselves today, no matter the season, there is an invitation to
faith-rest in the presence of Jesus. The Spirit's presence breathes
peace into our weary souls, and we drink from the refreshing
waters of his living love.

*Spirit, thank you for being my resting place at all times. You give
me respite from my enemies, and you lead me to refreshing
waters of peace. Thank you.*

FINAL WORDS

Joshua called together all the Israelites...and told them,
"I'm now very old and don't have much longer to live."

JOSHUA 23:2

*W*hen we perceive the end of a season drawing near, we can take advantage of the opportunity to reflect. As we look back over the lessons we've learned, the ways we've grown, and the difficulties we have faced, we may find that we have encouragement, direction, and wisdom to leave with those who remain.

Is there a transition that you are making? Do you want to move on mindfully, not just rushing ahead to the next thing? Let reflection move you toward gratitude. Write down the best moments, along with the worst, and their corresponding lessons. Think through what you want to take with you and what you want to leave behind. Let the Spirit of God lead you to the treasures of his wisdom, both on display and hidden in your story, and share it with those it will encourage.

Lord, I want to transition from different phases of life well and with purpose. Give me perspective to see what was done well and what could have been better. Thank you for the opportunity to learn and to share what I have learned with others.

GRACE OF GOD

"Yahweh your God has shown you his power and fought against your enemies for you. You have seen all the wonders that he has done...because he loves you."

JOSHUA 23:3

*H*ow have you seen the grace of God on display in your life? Has he shown you his power? Has he fought any battles for you? He moves in wonders, both big and small. He is as much at work in the details of your life as he is in your great areas of need.

As you spend time in the presence of God today, ask for his perspective to see where his loving acts of kindness are working in your life. Ask him to reveal where he has moved on your behalf. Ask him to show you where he has been sowing his mercy into the soil of your story. Where you recognize his goodness, let it be a salve of hope for your healing. Where you see his hand of mercy, let it encourage your heart to expect even more from his faithfulness. He is for you because he loves you.

Loving Father, you are the hope I hold on to. You are the vision I look at my life through. Reveal where you have worked, and where you are working still. I look to you.

BOLD FAITH

"Yahweh your God will absolutely keep his promises to you.
He will drive out all your enemies and make them retreat
before you so that you will possess their land."

JOSHUA 23:5

What the Lord promises, he will do. This promise is not tied to one person or even to one generation. Joshua was encouraging the Israelites that God would be faithful to his word. This did not depend on Joshua, and it did not depend on Moses before him, as the leaders over Israel. God's word to his people was and is his vow from generation to generation.

The promises of God are our courage. May they embolden our hearts and strengthen our spirits to walk ahead into greater things. There is more territory ahead of us to claim. There are more promises to be fulfilled. There is more hope ahead than any disappointment we leave behind. May we have the boldness of lions, confident in the strength of Christ in us. He will continue to fight for us and with us until we cross over into the realm of his eternal kingdom.

Yahweh, from generation to generation, you remain the same faithful God. I yield my life to you, to your will and ways. You are my God, and I cling to your promises. You are my courage and strength.

STRONG AND STEADFAST

"So be very strong and steadfast;
be careful to obey fully what is written
in the Scroll of the teaching of Moses,
without deviating from it."

JOSHUA 23:6

When we follow the Lord with our lives, giving him leadership rights to our destinies, we must lean on his grace to strengthen us along the way. We will not make it on our own. Left to our own strength, we may give up in order to remain within our comfort zones. We may try to build cities in deserts where we were only meant to pass through.

Let us lean on the everlasting kindness of our great God and Good Shepherd. As we follow his lead, obeying his kingdom laws above our own logic, and trusting in his wisdom over our flawed understanding of how the world works, we become strong and steadfast ones. The laws of the kingdom of Christ are for our benefit, just as the covenants of God are for our good. These pacts of partnership are filled with favor. He does not pull us into pain but into his pleasure. May we trust his heart as we persevere in faith.

Faithful One, I trust your leadership more than my own understanding. Guide me in your goodness and give me strength to keep following you.

WARNING AGAINST WANDERING WAYS

"Do not intermingle with the nations that are left among you nor speak the names of their gods when you take an oath. And by all means don't worship or pray to them."

JOSHUA 23:7

The mercy of God is powerful to save, to redeem, to restore, to heal, and to liberate us. Why would we look for our freedom in any other? Why would we honor others more than we honor our wonderful Savior? Christ is the fulfillment of every longing. He is the perfect portion.

Instead of finding our identity in what we do, who surrounds us, or our successes, may we look first, foremost, and continually to Jesus. The Spirit of God is our source of strength, help, and comfort. He is the power of God with us. There is no one greater in this world. Let us turn our eyes to the Lord as we begin our day, turn our hearts to him when we are troubled, and find the rest our souls long for in the peace of his presence. He is far better than any other promised goodness that the world has to offer.

Lord, when my heart begins to wander from you, will you direct me back to you with your still, small whisper? I worship you, for you are my God.

HEART SET ON YAHWEH

"As you have done until now,
cling tightly to Yahweh,
for he is your God."

JOSHUA 23:8

There are times when faith seems to come easily. When all is going well in our lives, why should we question the goodness of God? When we are living in the light of abundance, privilege, and passion, it is natural to delight in the favor we feel. And yet, we live in a world that is full of suffering and pain. We walk through as many shrouded valleys as we do glorious meadows and mountaintops.

Let us set our hearts on Yahweh and cling tightly to him, both in our seasons of lack and of plenty. He is a good Father through it all. His mercy is as palpable in our pain as it is in our peace. Let us hold tightly to our loving God. He is the steady anchor of our hope, keeping our hearts connected to his incredible power when we need a fresh dose of courage. He steadies our souls as we hold on to his unbreakable love.

My God, you are the one I cling to in both the good times and the hard. There is no one else like you in the heavens or on the earth. As I have done, so will I continue to do—I will hold on to you!

FAITH-FILLED PEOPLE

"Yahweh has driven out great and powerful nations before you!
No one was able to withstand you,
for Yahweh your God fights for you
as he promised he would!"

JOSHUA 23:9–10

We can be confident that when God calls us to move in faith, he goes with us. He faithfully moves in his powerful mercy to make a way through the barren wilderness. He goes to combat for us when we are in the fight of our lives. What he promises, he always follows through on.

We may not witness God as a cloud by day or a pillar of fire by night, as the wandering Israelites did. However, his power is as manifest through his Spirit. He moves in mighty miracles of mercy. Being a faith-filled person does not require super strength or highly tuned skill sets. All it requires is confident trust in who God is, in what he says, and in his faithfulness in carrying it out. When we are assured of his trustworthiness, we will courageously go where he leads and trust him to do what we cannot on our own. Our faith is based in him, not ourselves.

Yahweh, no one is able to withstand you when you move. Even a whisper sends the enemy fleeing. I put all my faith and trust in you, for you never ever fail!

RENEWED RELATIONSHIP

*"Above all else, keep watch over your hearts,
so as to always love Yahweh your God."*

JOSHUA 23:11

There are only two sources that truly know the state of our hearts: God and us. God sees through to the very root of every thought and intention. We can learn to know what our feelings and beliefs reveal about our faith in God. What are the fruits? If they align with the fruit of the Spirit, promoting humility, growth, and greater compassion, then we can rest assured that God is working in our hearts.

There are indicators that we can look for to signal us to when we are starting to drift from loving trust. When we have questions that crack the foundation of our belief systems, let's bring them to God. If left alone and ignored, they may erode the very framework of our faith. But when we let them drive us closer in connection with God, knowing that openness and hard conversations can deepen intimacy rather than threaten it, we will know his love even in our weakness. Let us connect heart to heart with the Spirit, knowing that vulnerability is the avenue to deeper relationship.

Spirit, you know my heart, and you see the reality of my feelings, questions, and convictions. May I find renewal in your fellowship today.

WORDS OF CAUTION

"But if you ever turn away...then you may be sure that Yahweh
your God will no longer drive them out before you.
Instead they will become a snare and a trap for you!"

JOSHUA 23:12–13

God does not protect us from the consequences of our choices.
He always mercifully works things together for those who love
him; this is true. But this does not mean that he removes the
consequences of our actions.

When we warn a child to not touch a hot stove, is it because we
are being controlling? By no means! We want to protect them from
the pain that they will experience. And yet, if that child touches
that hot stove, they will get burned. Do we ignore their cries? No,
we bandage their wounds and comfort them. But this does not
remove the sting or perhaps the scar that will remain. In the same
way, when God warns us against something and we choose to do
it anyway, there are natural consequences that follow. He is still
there to bind up our wounds, comfort us, and teach us. And yet,
we may have scars as a result.

*Jesus, thank you for your wisdom. I trust that you know better
than I do, and I submit to you. Thank you for your love that never
leaves, no matter what.*

REALIZE YOUR LIMITS

"Now I am about to go the way of all humanity."

JOSHUA 23:14

*N*one of us is invincible, and the time we have on this earth is like a morning mist. Soon enough, it will dissolve. How are we using the time that God has given us? How are we living this one beautiful, challenging life?

Perhaps you have found yourself caught up in the routines that blend one day into the next. Perhaps you have lost touch with the purpose you once felt. God is not finished with you yet. Every morning is a new opportunity to receive fresh, abundant mercy to flood you with light. Slow down and take a few moments to connect to the presence of God with you. Remember what it is that matters the most—the things that echo into eternity. Is it to love your family? Is it to reach out to your community? Connect with your purpose and do one thing to display it in your life today. This present moment is all you have, so make the most of it.

Lord, thank you for the reminder of the importance of intentionality in my life. I'm so grateful for your presence that shines through the fog of my circumstances. May my choices, my life, and my love bring you glory.

WONDERFUL GOD

"You know with all your heart and soul that
not one promise of Yahweh your God has failed."

JOSHUA 23:14

*W*hat is it that you know that you know that you know about
God? There are things that are so central to our beliefs that they
go to the very depths of our beings—"all [our] heart and soul." The
way he moves in our lives is so unique, and yet the characteristics
he displays are the same. The fruit of his Spirit is always evident in
the lives of his beloved ones.

Not one promise of Yahweh has failed. He's not going to change
now. What he has vowed, he will fulfill. What he set out to do, he
will complete. May we rest in the confidence of his unfailing nature
and plant ourselves on the solid rock of his faithfulness. He is more
wonderful than words can express. He is more loyal than the rising
sun. Let's set our hopes on him, for he is constant and true, and he
will always be.

*Wonderful One, thank you for your unending love, your consistent
kindness, and the reliability of your Word. All my hope is in you!
May my heart and soul trust you and know the incomparable
expanse of your goodness.*

COVENANT KEEPERS

"If you break the covenant our God, Yahweh, made with you
and worship other gods and bow down to them,
his anger will blaze against you."

JOSHUA 23:16

How dependable is your word? How consistent are you with your promises? We are all human, and we all fall short of the glory of God—that's why we need a Savior! Jesus is the Anointed One, our liberator "from the guilt, punishment, and power of sin" (Romans 3:23–24). This is no small thing. In the mercy of Christ, the anger of God is satisfied. He does not hold against us what Christ has already taken care of.

And yet, our word matters. As lovers of God, keeping the promises we make is important. Though we are not perfect, let us work to be consistent. When we fail, let us repent and try again. Let's surround ourselves with the help we need, the accountability that will challenge us, and move things around in our lives to keep the covenants we have made. More than anything, let's lean on Jesus and his merciful strength, for he is our perfection and our covering.

Great God, thank you for providing everything I need to follow you. You overwhelm my faith with your faithfulness, and you never break your covenant. How I love you!

HISTORY TEACHES US

"This is what Yahweh the God of Israel has to say to you: 'Long ago, your forefathers—Terah, father of Abraham and father of Nahor—lived beyond the Euphrates and worshiped other gods.'"

JOSHUA 24:2

When we look through history, we must not only look at the triumphs and victories but also at the defeats and failures. We must learn from the errors of those who have gone before us and recognize the same tendencies in ourselves. We cannot separate ourselves as superior, thinking we are above making the same mistakes. We are only human, after all.

May we have the courage to look at the dark parts of our history, in our families, cities, nations, and in the world. As we face them, we may also recognize similarities in ourselves. This is so important! If we will humble ourselves before the Lord and let him shine the light of his truth on the shadows of our hearts, we can then be transformed in the light of his mercy. May his kindness lead us to repentance, and may we humbly admit our continual need for his grace to choose the path of his love.

Merciful One, I humbly open my heart to you. I want to be soft to your correction and moved by your compassion toward others. Speak, Lord.

FROM BARRIERS TO BREAKTHROUGH

"I freed your forefathers from Egypt and brought you to the Red Sea, but the Egyptians pursued them with chariots and horsemen."

JOSHUA 24:6

The mercy of God led the Israelites out of their captivity in Egypt. By his power, he split the Red Sea so that they could cross over ahead of the great army pursuing them. When God leads us, he will provide a way where there doesn't seem to be any. When he liberates us, he will not stop until we are completely free.

When we experience the beginnings of liberation, we may be discouraged when we come up against seemingly impossible obstacles. But that is never the end. Let us not turn back toward our captivity, to the way things were before. Let's look ahead, straight into the face of the barrier in front of us. That is where our miracle lies. That is where God will do what only he can do by his power. When we follow him, we can trust him to clear a path. He will do it.

Almighty God, make a way where I can see none. I have followed you this far, and I won't stop now. You are my freedom fighter, and I trust you!

STAY STRONG

"Then our people cried out to Yahweh for help,
and he put a thick, dark cloud between you and the Egyptians…
You saw with your own eyes what I did to the Egyptians."

JOSHUA 24:7

Our strength is not found in our own problem-solving skills or in the power of our positivity. Our true strength comes from God. When we are weak, his power is made even more evident in our lives. Let's not be afraid to cry out to Yahweh for help when we need it. He is a ready and proven help in times of trouble. He is more than enough and always available when we need him, just like the psalmist wrote (Psalm 46:1).

When you see no way out of the trouble you are in, call out to God. He is near. When you are overwhelmed by the inability to escape your enemies, cry out to him, for he is your Advocate and your defense. He will move on your behalf. So stay strong, not by ignoring your troubles but by calling on the Lord for his help.

Mighty God, when I have no other hope, you are my strong and ready help. You deliver me from my fears and lead me into my freedom. Thank you.

POWERFUL PROTECTOR

"I refused to listen to Balaam.
Instead he had to prophesy my blessings over you!
I rescued you from his power."

JOSHUA 24:10

*Y*ahweh is more influential than any other powers or principalities or any king or kingdoms in the earth. He causes those who seek to curse his people to bless them instead. Just as God did this for Israel, he will do it for you. He will turn curses into blessings, and the power of another's hatred toward you will be rendered helpless in his overwhelming love.

God is our rescuer. Jesus is our Savior. He is our liberator and our loving leader. He will not let the darkness of another extinguish the light that we carry. The Spirit of God is our life-source and strength, and no one can take that away from us. No one can tear us apart from his love—nothing can come between his mercy and our lives. Even when nations rage, he keeps us in the peace of his heart. What he has done before, he will do again. He will come through as we cry out to him for help.

Almighty One, no one can turn the hearts of men the way that you can. Protect me from the harmful intentions of others and keep me close to your love.

NOTHING IMPOSSIBLE

"Later, after you crossed the Jordan miraculously,
you faced another impossibility—
Jericho!...I gave you victory over them all!"

JOSHUA 24:11

*H*ow often do we get through one hard situation only to encounter another shortly after? There are times when it feels as if the skies have opened and a deluge of problems rain down over us. Does this mean we have upset God? Does it mean that we have somehow gone astray? Let us remember that God's Word never says that our lives will be easy. Every impossibility is an opportunity for a great miracle.

Take courage when hard times come, for God is faithful, and he will faithfully lead you through them all. His loyal love never leaves you. He is the same miracle working God today as he was when the Red Sea opened and the walls of Jericho came tumbling down. Take heart, for the Lord your God is victorious over every obstacle and every battle, and nothing is impossible for him.

Great God, I know that nothing is impossible for you. I cling to you in hope, trusting you to faithfully lead me through each and every trial I face. You are my victory, and I follow you.

ABUNDANT LIFE

"You are now living in the land I gave you. You are eating grapes
from vines that others planted and olives from trees planted by the
people who lived there before you."

JOSHUA 24:13

The Lord leads us into goodness. He is wonderful in his provision,
and he is abundant in his gift-giving. If we haven't yet entered
into the plenty of his promises, let us keep going, for we have not
reached the end.

Where we are experiencing the abundance of God's life in ours,
may we not withhold the gratitude of our hearts. Let's live with
the same generosity that he displays toward us. Let's not take
for granted where we came from or the struggles we've walked
through. The garden of God's favor is plentiful, and there is more
than enough to feed our hungry hearts. He is so very wonderful,
and he is a never-ending source of fresh hope, life, and joy. He is
our portion; let us rejoice in the limitlessness of his love.

*Faithful Father, thank you for the abundance of your love that is
always overflowing. I don't take for granted the plenty of your
presence. I love you!*

THE CHOICE IS YOURS

"Now therefore, worship Yahweh with holy awe and serve him in authentic love and loyalty. Remove from your hearts every false god to whom your fathers bowed down...and serve Yahweh."

JOSHUA 24:14

It is our choice how we will live our lives. It is up to us to decide the values by which we will live. Will we serve Yahweh with holy awe, surrendering our very lives to him? Will we follow along the path of his laid-down-love, where Jesus leads the way? If we truly love him, then our lives will show it.

Love is active, and it continually refines us. Love is a choice, and it is continually made or rejected. We are not faultless, and we never will be. But when we are yielded to the love of God, we give him the right to instruct, correct, and guide us. How does this show up in our lives? Are we choosing to worship God with our whole selves? Do we have fellowship with him? Today is another opportunity to decide for ourselves whom we will serve.

Yahweh, thank you for the autonomy of choice. I want to reflect you in the way I live, the way I love, and the way I relate to others. May my life be a fragrant offering of worship to you.

FULLY EMBRACE GOD

*"I and my family, we will give our lives
to worship and serve Yahweh!"*

JOSHUA 24:15

*E*very one of us gets to choose whom we will serve. Whether we live for our own interests or for a greater purpose is up to us—and what that greater purpose is also depends on our choices. When we fully embrace God with our lives, giving him the worship and honor he deserves, we align ourselves with his kingdom.

The kingdom of God is eternal, full of light, love, and truth. There is wisdom beyond our understanding and resources of joy, hope, and grace to fill our lives. There is so much more available in God than we could provide for ourselves. May we press into his presence, seeking to live by his kingdom ways above our own. Whatever we do, may we know that we get to choose, and it's never too late to choose differently.

Yahweh, you know my strengths and my weaknesses. Nothing about me is hidden from you. I want to choose your ways over my own. Empower me by your Spirit to live according to your kingdom's wisdom.

WORSHIP HIM

"We, too, will worship and serve Yahweh,
for he alone is our God."

JOSHUA 24:18

In the context of community, we can be encouraged by the power of God in each other's lives. When we share our lives with one another, being open about our triumphs and our struggles, we lean on each other through the good and the bad. As we watch the tenacity of others' faith in choosing to surrender to God and to love others, even when it is difficult, does our own faith not also strengthen?

When we see how faithfully God works in the hills and valleys of those around us, may we also be encouraged to keep worshiping and serving God. He alone is Savior. He alone is Redeemer. He is unrelenting in devoted love and uninterrupted in marvelous mercy. By his grace, we are strengthened in faith as we continue to worship God in the fellowship of his family.

My God, awe and thanksgiving arise within me as I watch what you do for others who love and serve you. I won't hold back my life from you, for you are faithful and true. I worship you!

HOLY GOD

Joshua warned the people, "Don't be so quick to say,
'We will worship and serve Yahweh,' for he is a holy God.
And he will tolerate no rivals."

JOSHUA 24:19

The holiness of God separates him from all darkness. No shadows are present in his love, for he is pure light and truth. As we worship God, his light shines on our lives, so let's be ready to submit every shadow to his glorious mercy and not hide a single thing from him. God cannot be tricked. He knows our hearts through and through. If we intend to serve him, he knows it. If we intend to only have the appearance of serving him but not offer him our hearts, he also knows that.

First John 1:5–6 says, "God is pure light. You will never find even a trace of darkness in him. If we claim that we share life with him, but keep walking in the realm of darkness, we're fooling ourselves and not living the truth." This echoes Joshua's warning to the Israelites. If we are going to live for God, it should be with the full intention of living in his life-giving light. He is holy, and darkness has no place in him.

Holy God, shine the light of your truth on my heart. Refine me as I open up to you.

Purging Our Hearts

"Now then," said Joshua, "throw away these foreign gods that are among you, and yield your hearts fully to Yahweh the God of Israel!"

JOSHUA 24:23

When we look at our lives, may we look with the discernment of God's wisdom. Are there any hidden idols shoved into our closets? Are there any areas of our lives that we purposefully keep from the sight of others lest we be found out? Let's bring it all out in the open, into the light of God's truth. He meets us with mercy whenever we yield our hearts to him.

It is important that we take the time to look through the halls of our hearts for hidden compromise. Is there anything that has not been submitted to the love of Christ? Is there anything that we have kept to ourselves, not wanting to know what he truly thinks? Let's throw away the things that hinder us from his love. Let's get rid of everything that claims its self-importance and keeps us from walking in the freedom of Christ's life-giving mercy. A spring-cleaning of the heart does us good.

Jesus, you are the Light of the World, and you are the light of my life. I yield my heart to you fully; I give you access to every part of me.

FULL HEARTS OF SURRENDER

The people promised Joshua,
"We really will worship and serve our God, Yahweh,
and listen to his voice."

JOSHUA 24:24

*W*orshiping the Lord isn't just about what we say, do, or feel. It is about true, living relationship. When we serve him, it is not like those who serve an indifferent or demanding master. He knows us fully, and he longs that we should know him as he is. Listening to his voice is an important part of relationship.

How well do we recognize the voice of our Father? Do we know the tone and the texture of his voice as well as we know what he says? As we get to know him in Spirit and in truth, as he leads us in loving-kindness, we will get to know the feel of his voice in our own spirit. With full hearts of surrender, we give him access to refine, to instruct, and to rearrange our priorities. May we spend time worshiping him, serving him, and, most of all today, listening to his voice.

Worthy One, I want to know the tone of your voice and the fruit of your Word. Speak to me and instruct me with your gentle wisdom. Your love is better than life, and I want to know you more.

RENEWED COVENANT

On that day when the people were gathered at Shechem,
Joshua made a covenant between them and Yahweh,
which contained laws the people were to obey.

JOSHUA 24:25

*Y*ahweh is a God of covenant. He made a covenant with
Noah, with Abraham, and with the people of Israel. They were
solemn vows of God's promise to humankind through a chosen
partnership. The covenant between Israel and Yahweh included
laws that the people were to obey.

In Jesus Christ, each of these covenants has been fulfilled. He has
established a new covenant where we come to the Father directly
through him. He is the all-sufficient sacrifice, and he sits on the
mercy-seat. We approach him and find the forgiveness of all our
sins in his love. We surrender our lives to him, and he leads us into
his life. There is nothing that separates us from his love, and he has
given us freedom. The law of Moses condemns, but the law of
love sets us free, and we are free indeed.

*Jesus, thank you for making a new covenant with us and for
removing condemnation from our lives under your love. I am in
awe of you.*

CREATED TO WITNESS

Joshua said to all the people, "Look at this stone!
It will serve as a witness, for it heard all the words
that Yahweh spoke to us."

JOSHUA 24:27

*E*ven the stones bear witness to the words that God speaks. Creation stands as an eyewitness to what God does. If they recognize his power, how much more should we? Let's actively recall the goodness of our God. Let's remember what he has already done and stand upon the foundation of his faithfulness as we look to our future.

All of nature is the handiwork of God. Let us look for evidence of his mercy in the world around us. There are lessons to be found of God's character through the cycles of the earth. There are clues to his kingdom through the changing seasons. In the cosmos, there are wonders to cause us to marvel at the magnitude of the greatness God. In our awe of creation, let us not forget that we are image bearers—how much more is God working in us!

Creator, give me eyes to see the mysteries of your wonderful nature within the universe. As my heart fills with wonder, I remember: not only do the stars speak of your majesty, but so do I.

SERVANT OF GOD

Some time later, Joshua son of Nun, the servant of Yahweh,
died at the age of one hundred and ten.

JOSHUA 24:29

Joshua faithfully served Yahweh as Israel's warrior-chief. He led Israel with strength and with courage to conquer all their enemies. He did not count his own life as too important; rather, he sought God in all things, not only on his own behalf, but also on behalf of the whole nation. He was a prophet and a leader, foreshadowing the leadership of Christ.

Joshua brought Israel into a new era of its history. They went from wilderness wanderers to courageous conquerors. We have the same hope. Jesus leads us from our own wilderness seasons into new territories of abundance, but we must be brave and trust in his leadership. He will not fail us, just as he never failed Joshua or Israel. He gives us everything we need, including the power of his presence that fights on our behalf. May we follow him with faith, for he will never fail.

Jesus, you are the leader I submit to. I am your willing and ready servant. Speak to me, lead me, and move in mighty ways as we venture into the unknown together.

FAITHFUL LIVES

Israel was faithful to serve Yahweh during the lifetime of Joshua and the lifetime of the elders who lived on after Joshua, those who had experienced all the miracles that Yahweh had done for Israel.

JOSHUA 24:31

There is something about living in the undeniable mercy of God that keeps us connected to God through faith. His faithfulness encourages us to be faithful. We draw assurance from the courage we find in his tangible presence. When he moves in mighty miracles, how could we deny his power?

No matter our experience of God's power in our lives, may we faithfully serve him with open hearts that long to know him more. He is always moving, so let's look for where he is already working. May we gain courage from others who have experienced his power. May we continually press into his presence for more. Relationship with God through his Spirit is ours, so let's not hesitate to turn to him with all of our questions and longings. He is so very faithful; let's build our lives on his solid foundation, living for his purposes.

Yahweh, I will not forget what you have done. I will live for you, for you are better than any other. Keep me close to you as I live yielded to your love.

June

TRANSITION

After Joshua died, the twelve tribal leaders consulted Yahweh for a prophetic sign and asked, "Which tribe do you choose to be the first to lead the attack against the Canaanites?"

JUDGES 1:1

Change is guaranteed in our lives. We will constantly navigate the shifting of people, jobs, expectations, and responsibilities throughout our lifetime. No matter how predictably or how suddenly a change comes, may we turn to God and rest in the confidence of his sovereignty.

In times of transition in our lives, we can always go to God for wisdom and direction. There is nothing that surprises him. He always has a plan of redemption for us—even in the greatest tragedies. May we find courage and peace in his wise guidance, for he is with us through every dilemma we face. Let's lean on his understanding, for it is expansive and full of loving truth.

Lord, you are the one I lean on in times of calm, and you are the one I look to in times of uncertainty. Lead me with your love and speak your truth to my heart. Fill me with courage to keep going, trusting your faithfulness every step of the way.

ANSWERED AND DIRECTED

Yahweh answered them, "Let Judah take the lead.
I have delivered the land into their hands."

JUDGES 1:2–3

When we seek the Lord for answers, he provides them. He directs us with his confident truth. Though he may not always answer as specifically as we would like, his directives can be like a river of grace. As we rest in his love, we do what we know to do, and he course corrects as we continue to follow him. He is faithful to guide us.

When you face a proverbial fork in the road, do you go to God first? As you wait upon him, his presence expands your awareness of his love. Everything he does is from a full heart of loving-kindness. He guides us with his wisdom, and he sees everything clearly. We can trust his intentions, and we can rest in the confidence of his unfailing character. Go to him with all your questions and wait for his answer.

Yahweh, I look to you for answers and direction. Move my heart as I listen for your voice. Speak clearly and direct me with your Spirit. I love you!

AGREEMENT

Judah then enlisted support from their brother-tribe Simeon, saying, "Follow us into our territory and fight with us against the Canaanites; then we will do the same for you." So the Simeonites agreed and joined them.

JUDGES 1:3

When we go into battles that are too big for us to handle on our own, instead of shrinking back in fear, may we look for help and agreement. We were made for community; we need each other. There's no need to walk into an overwhelming circumstance hoping for the best on our own. We find courage and confidence in the solidarity and help of others.

The help we seek can also be mutually beneficial. When someone comes to our aid, are we not much more willing to return the favor? If there is a situation where you feel in over your head, look at who is in your life that you could ask assistance from. Know that in so doing, you can also offer them help in their own battles.

Gracious God, thank you for the power of community. I want to know the blessing of fellowship through the agreement of help in my life and in others' lives. May I look for ways to incorporate the strength of the body of Christ rather than relying on my own strength. Thank you!

YAHWEH GIVES VICTORY

When Judah advanced,
Yahweh gave them victory over the Canaanites and Perizzites,
and they defeated ten thousand men at Bezek.

JUDGES 1:4

*A*s Judah advanced to take their God-given inheritance, they had the favor of the Lord on their side. Whenever we move forward to claim the promises that God has given us, we also know that we walk in the favor of the Lord. He is the one who gives us victory, and he supports us in our endeavors. Whenever we walk in the confidence of his Word, we can know that God is also fighting for us.

Battles are not without struggle. So as we move into the realm of our promised inheritance, we will have battles to fight and win. May we not be discouraged when there is pushback, and may we not give up when we are required to fight through the doubts of others. When things are tough, it does not mean that God is not with us. He is fighting for us, and we will know victory in and through him.

Lord, you are my confidence and my strength. You give victory, and I will not be afraid when battles rage. You are my support through it all. I trust you.

SEEK THE BLESSING

"Please, give me a blessing," she replied. "I know you've already given me some arid desert land, but please give me a field with springs of water." So Caleb blessed her with a field that had both upper and lower springs.

JUDGES 1:15

*C*aleb's response to his daughter's request is reflective of how our good Father responds to our appeals. He is a loving Father who loves to give good gifts. Even though the request came from the pressure of her husband, when Achsah asked her father for a better plot of land, he blessed her with it.

May we have the confidence of dearly loved children as we come to our Father through Christ. He has plentiful springs of living water to refresh us. His resources are endless, and he delights to honor our requests with his blessing. May we not hold back our petitions, knowing that God is good. He is kind and thoughtful, and he will not withhold from us that which will benefit our lives, our souls, and our relationships. Let's seek his blessing today.

Loving Father, I will not withhold my request for more from you today. I know that you have already blessed me, and I am so grateful. Even more, I am thankful that there's always more available in your kingdom.

PRESENCE AND POWER

Yahweh's presence and power were with the men of Judah and they were able to conquer the hill country.

JUDGES 1:19

*T*he presence and power of God is our breakthrough. What we could never accomplish on our own, the Spirit of God does through us. He is our strength, our shield, and our defense. He is the authority that breaks down strongholds and makes a path in the dry bed of the sea. God's presence is his power, and his presence is always available through his Spirit.

With the Spirit as our empowering strength, we are able to conquer our enemies. The lies that would cause us to shrink in shame are made powerless in the overcoming truth of our identity as sons and daughters of the living God. With the presence and power of Jesus, every trial becomes an opportunity for growth, every battle becomes a place of breakthrough, and every question becomes a directive for the wisdom of God to meet it.

All-powerful One, your presence is all I need. I long to live consciously in the strength, courage, and confidence of your presence with me. I rely on you in all things.

DEALING WITH EVERY ISSUE

The tribe of Benjamin, however, failed to conquer the Jebusites living in Jerusalem. So to this day, the Jebusites live among the Benjamites in Jerusalem.

JUDGES 1:21

When we do not deal with every issue within our hearts, we leave room for the same patterns of defeat to repeat in our lives. When we leave little places of compromise in our lifestyles, they will prevent us from possessing our full inheritance in Christ. How thorough are we in eliminating every evil from our lives?

It's time to take our habits seriously. How prone are we to seething anger, forms of hatred, cursing, and lying? Do we allow the desire for wealth to undermine our integrity? Have we grown accustomed to our secret sins, looking for ways to continue in them? May we lay aside our old selves, where we tried to hide our guilt, and instead live in the life-giving light of Christ in us. He has made us new, and he continues to transform us into his image as we submit our lives to him. We are new creations in Christ, so let's be sure to deal with every issue that competes with the power of his love in our lives.

Jesus, I yield my heart and life to you. Transform me in your regenerative love. I keep nothing hidden from you.

AREAS OF COMPROMISE

> Whenever Israel gained the upper hand,
> they subjected the Canaanites to forced labor;
> but they did not completely drive them out.
>
> JUDGES 1:28

When we do not completely drive out the enemies of our peace in Christ, we set ourselves up for a continued struggle. Are there any cycles that you have not been liberated from? Perhaps it's time to stop looking at the cycle and instead look at the areas of compromise that lead to the cyclical behavior.

The power of Christ sets us free. We have been given new life in him, and our identity as children of the Most High overwhelms every other identity that we have known before. Still, how we live matters. What we allow in our lives will become areas of possibility. Instead of using our freedom to live in the light of Christ, will we use it to excuse our lack of accountability? May we embrace the liberty of love and move in the power of our choices.

Wise One, thank you for stooping to meet us wherever we are. I don't want to compromise my freedom in you. Empower me to face the compromises in my life and submit them to your truth and wisdom.

PUSHBACK

The tribe of Dan was least successful.
The Amorites forced them back into the hills
and they could no longer live in the valley.

JUDGES 1:34

*T*here may be times in our lives where the enemy pushes us back into retreat for a season. This is not the end of the battle though. In Christ, our ultimate victory over every foe is secure. The redemptive power of Christ covers every area of our lives, including our failures.

If you find yourself in a time where you are getting tremendous pushback where you had once gained territory, don't let despair set in. In your disappointment, look to God. He is with you, and he has the perspective you need. He sits above the clouds with perfect vision. Let him speak his truth over your situation and trust what he says. Sometimes pushback is feeling the tension of a slingshot. Though you may be moving back, it is from that place that God will propel you forward at the right time.

Redeemer, I am so thankful for your power in my life. I'm so grateful that even my failures are turned into fodder for your glorious redemption. Move in my life, Lord. I trust you.

STRENGTH TO OVERCOME

When the descendants of Joseph grew stronger,
they overpowered the Amorites and ruled over them.

JUDGES 1:35

*A*fter the tribe of Dan was pushed back into the hills for a time, they grew strong in anticipation of reclaiming their land. They did not idly sit in resignation, but they trained and prepared to retake their inheritance.

May we, too, find strength to overcome despondency. Are there areas of defeat in our lives that have caused us to retreat? In our recovery, which will include some disappointment, grief, and questioning, may we not forget the importance of rest. When we have taken some space and time, we will need to actively train with the vision of moving forward once more. When we grow stronger, then we will be able to overpower and overcome our enemies. With Christ himself as our companion, his strength will infuse our weakness and lead us into our victory at just the right time. May we press into him as we pursue our healing.

Christ, you are my strength and my support. Encourage my heart as you minister your peace and wisdom in your presence. With you, I know that I can overcome any foe.

HOLY REBUKE

"I said, 'I will never, never break my covenant with you,
and you are never, never to make a covenant with the
inhabitants of this land'...But you have not listened to my voice.
See what you have done!"

JUDGES 2:1–2

*T*he Lord's promise to never break his covenant is as sure as his character. He is unfailing and unmoving in intention. What he says he will do, he does. He rescued Israel from Egypt, and he moved in signs and miracle-wonders throughout their time in the desert and into the promised land.

When the Lord vowed to never break his covenant, he also instructed his people to never make a covenant with those who dwelled in the lands that they were conquering. God takes covenants seriously; they are his word. He also knows the power of covenants with others. He could not nullify a promise that others had made. May we take the Lord at his word and trust that what he instructs us in has purpose. May we trust him more than we trust ourselves. And when he rebukes us, may we be quick to respond.

Lord, I know that your ways are higher than my own. I know that you know best. Forgive me for how I have rebelled against your Word and restore me in your kindness.

CONSEQUENCES

"Therefore listen to what I'm telling you—I won't drive them out
before you. Instead, they will be thorns in your sides,
and their gods will become a trap for you!"

JUDGES 2:3

*W*e cannot escape the consequences of our choices. There are
some things that, in our choosing, change our trajectories. God is
ultimately a God of redemption. He can use anything, including
our wandering ways and rebellious tendencies, to bring about
beauty. When we submit our lives to Christ, our shame is covered,
and we are made new. But that does not mean that there are no
natural effects of the choices that led us there.

When we yield our hearts and lives to the Lord, he gives us his
Spirit. He promises to make all things new, but this does not mean
that we escape responsibility for wrongs we have committed. May
we humbly follow the Lord, and when we turn to him, know that
he will empower us by his strength to walk in humility and love.
Even when thorns persist in our lives, the Spirit of God persists
even more steadily.

*Faithful One, thank you for the reminder that my choices matter.
May my heart remain humble as I seek restoration in relationships
where I have wounded others. Thank you for your help.*

PIERCED HEARTS

After the Angel of Yahweh had delivered his message to all the Israelites, the people burst out with loud, bitter weeping.

JUDGES 2:4

*W*hen we are rebuked by the truth of the Lord, reminded of how faithful he is and yet how regularly we distrust him, how could our hearts not be pierced? He is the God of our salvation, and he leads us in confidence and kindness. And how do we repay him? We forget the goodness of his love, and we compromise our own by making vows with those who do not have our best interest at heart.

It is right for us to mourn our own wandering ways when they are brought to light. With hearts that are convicted of God's truth and our own inability to live by it, we are directed back to the redemptive love of Christ. He is our salvation, the only pure and lasting sacrifice, and our hope. May we grieve what we need to grieve in ourselves as we face the consequences of our choices and take his hand once again. He is still our loving leader.

Jesus, when I realize how little I trust you and your word, I am pierced to the very core. Forgive me for my selfish ways. I want to walk in submission to your love that is better than life.

REPENTANT SACRIFICE

They named that place Bokim,
and in that place of tears they offered sacrifices to Yahweh.

JUDGES 2:5

*J*esus' sacrifice is sufficient for us in every circumstance, and in every turning of our hearts toward God. His salvation is eternal, and his hope is for all who believe. When we repent and return to him, there is nothing more to add to his sacrifice. We do not burn grains or offer lambs, for he has already paid the highest price.

As we offer our hearts as plots for God's seeds to grow, may we come with humility. He is our gardener, the one who tends to the soil of our surrender. What he plants in us will thrive under the light of his leadership. We allow him to guide us in willing surrender, trusting that his truth stands firm and his faithfulness will never waver. What a wonderful and blessed hope we have every time we turn and return to God.

Savior, thank you for your sacrifice that once and for all covered the sin of all humankind. As I turn to you with a humble and repentant heart, I know that you receive me. You are my God, and I will follow you.

RESTORED TO CONQUER

Joshua released the people to go take possession
of their territorial inheritance.

JUDGES 2:6

After the people of Israel were confronted by the truth of God, they responded with grief and with repentance. They offered sacrifices that demonstrated their longing for restoration. And how did God, through Joshua, respond? He sent them out to conquer their inheritance once again.

God did not revoke the Israelites' inheritance, and he won't do that with us either. What he has promised, he will faithfully fulfill. When we are restored in connection and fellowship with God, we are empowered to go into our destinies with his presence. With our relationship repaired, we walk in the confidence of submitted trust. May we continually surrender ourselves to the leadership of our faithful Father, for he will never change. Let us forge ahead into the promises of his kingdom as he releases us to do so. We have been restored in Christ to conquer our enemies and to claim our inheritance in him.

Restorer, thank you for doing all that needed to be done in order for me to know you. I come to you with humble submission. Do what only you can do and redeem even my greatest failures.

UNDENIABLE POWER

The people faithfully worshiped Yahweh all the days of Joshua
and through all the days of the elders who outlived him.
They had all experienced the many astounding miracles
Yahweh had done for Israel.

JUDGES 2:7

It is impossible to deny the power of God when you have lived
through it. The Israelites, who were delivered out of their captivity
in Egypt, who were led by the cloud and pillar in the desert, who
saw cities crumble and the sun stand still, could not explain away
the astounding miracles they had experienced time and again.

Their faith was their own, for they experienced the mighty power
of God and saw his signs and wonders for themselves. These
people faithfully worshiped Yahweh, for they knew him and knew
what he was like. He had become real to them, not just an ideal
passed down through stories. They worshiped Yahweh because he
was *their* God. He was the one they depended on. He was their
leader. Do we worship God out of a living relationship with him?
May we know the foundation of our faith, and yet may we build
upon it in surrendered relationship.

*God, you are my God. Reveal yourself to me as I walk hand in
hand with you. I honor and worship you with my life.*

FORGOTTEN WONDERS

Eventually, after that entire generation died and was buried, the next generation forgot Yahweh and all that he had done for Israel.

JUDGES 2:10

*A*s one generation passed away and another rose to adulthood, they lost their way. They forgot the wonders that God had performed in the wilderness. They no longer remembered the manna or the split-open rock that gave them water. They failed to recall the miraculous parting of the Jordan when Israel was readying to cross into the promised land. They forgot the walls of Jericho falling down, the sun standing still, and the way God empowered them to conquer their foes.

It is easy for the second generation of a movement to forget the truth and power of the first generation. They may idolize the memories and yet fail to apply the same power that is available to them to advance in the ways of God. There are no dead-ends in the kingdom of God. There is always more to pursue, always more to discover, and always more to grow in. May we press into the pursuit of God's presence with us and apply the wisdom of previous generations to our lives.

Yahweh, I know that you are unchanging. You still move in power, and you move in signs and wonders. I press in to know you more.

FALLING AWAY

The Israelites did what was evil the sight of Yahweh
and worshiped the images of Baal.

JUDGES 2:11

*W*hen we lose our connection to God, we inevitably replace
the importance of that relationship with a substitute. When the
Israelites wandered from Yahweh's leadership, they began to
worship the images of the Canaanite gods. Living among them,
they intermingled and began to believe what the Canaanites
believed. They took on Canaanite customs and forgot the power
of their connection to the God of Israel.

There is no true substitute for God. He is the fulfillment of every
longing, of every need, and of every living thing. He is the perfect
representation of mercy and justice. He is the God who fights
for his people. He is the God who mercifully restores them time
and again. Even if we have found ourselves elevating other things
above Yahweh, it is not too late to return to him. He is always
within reach, and his power is always ready to restore us.

*Great God, nothing and no one compares to you. Your love is
greater than anything. I turn to you, and I lay down the idols that I
have put before you. Restore me in your mercy.*

WANDERING HEARTS

Israel deserted Yahweh, the God of their ancestors, who had rescued them from Egypt. They found new gods to worship— the gods of the people around them.

JUDGES 2:12

*N*one of us is immune to the pull of the culture around us. Our upbringing does not guarantee the trajectory of our lives. No matter how wonderfully faithful our parents have been, their faith is not our faith. We make our own choices, and we get to direct our hearts according to our own ways.

What kind of faith marks our lives? Do we live under the guise of tradition and yet throw away the importance of our personal choices? Though Israel deserted Yahweh, it is important that we recognize that God never deserted Israel. No matter how far we have wandered, God has not abandoned us. He is close, and so is his help. Whenever we humble our hearts and turn to him, he is there. Even in our wandering, we cannot wander outside the realm of his mercy.

Yahweh, I don't want to wander from you and your ways. When I find myself adopting values that don't align with yours, remind me of your incomparable goodness.

NEAR DESTRUCTION

> Every time they went into battle, Yahweh raised his hand
> against them to their undoing, just as he had warned them,
> and they were in great distress.
>
> JUDGES 2:15

How closely do we listen to God? Do we take his warnings as seriously as we do his goodness? He is full of wisdom, and he will not withhold his truth from us when we seek it. When we are not in right relationship with him, we should not expect his peace to keep us.

In our undoing, may we turn to God. When our hopes and our expectations fall apart, let's come home to him. Have we forgotten what he spoke to us? If so, it is never too late to heed his voice. It is never too late to live by his truth. If, however, we are living for the Lord in close relationship and walking his path of love, we should not fear the destruction that feels as if it's closing in around us. Not all trials and troubles are evidence of our wandering. In all things, especially in our distress, may we turn to our merciful Lord.

Great God, when my life is out of control and I cannot get my footing, rise up beneath me. I yield to your wisdom and truth.

MERCIFUL GOD

Yahweh raised up deliverers from among them
who rescued them from the marauding bands.

JUDGES 2:16

*E*ven when we are far from the Lord, he makes merciful provisions for us. He raises up rescuers among the living, and he leads us to his heart through their direction. When we have forgotten who he is, he still reaches out in loyal love. He still provides a path of restoration and redemption for us.

Christ is our great deliverer. He is the almighty restorer, our holy hope, and our saving grace. He rescues us from those who overpower us. He leads us out of our error and bondage into glorious freedom. There is no other who can claim the same power, and no one else can cover our sin with grave-robbing authority. Jesus is the image of the merciful Father, the living expression of love, and our path to eternal freedom. Where there is hopelessness in your heart, look to Jesus, for he is your heavenly liberator in every season and circumstance.

Jesus, you are my Savior, and I depend on your mercy to rescue me. You are my holy hope, and I surrender in your love to your ways. You are worthy of my very life.

COMMISSIONED TO DELIVER

Whenever Yahweh raised up a hero for them, his presence and power were with that leader, and he would rescue the people from their enemies as long as that deliverer lived.

JUDGES 2:18

The Lord is relentless in love and mercy. He faithfully raised up champion-deliverers within Israel to lead them back to himself. He used these heroes of the faith to rescue the people from their adversaries. As long as they lived, the presence and power of God was with these deliverers.

When we are submitted to God and his purposes, he empowers us with his Spirit to do his work. He not only leads us into his kingdom, but he uses us to lead others there as well. He uses our willingness to deliver those who are captive in their sin and shame by pointing them to our true deliverer, Jesus. He is the fullness of God's presence and power with us. The Spirit moves in mighty acts of wonder as we yield our lives to him. He delivers us from the power of our enemies, and he liberates us from our fears.

Lord, you are my champion-deliverer. Use my life to display your presence and power. May all I do be reflective of my humble submission to you. I love you!

IMPERFECT PEOPLE

When their champion died, then the people would relapse into their former idolatry. They would...refuse to give up their evil ways.

JUDGES 2:19

When we look through the history of Israel, it is not only their wandering that we see on display; it is our own missteps reflected back to us. The Scriptures are full of imperfect people, and we are no different. May we be like the generations who turned back to Yahweh when they had the opportunity instead of relapsing into our former idolatrous ways.

Even when we do fall back into old patterns and habits that don't serve us well, let alone serve God, his mercy is always reaching toward us. It is not perfection that God is after—it is willing and humble hearts. May we choose today to turn away from our selfish tendencies that lack love and integrity and submit our hearts and lives once again to the greater kingdom ways of Jesus Christ, our Redeemer and living hope.

Loving Lord, I'm so grateful for your mercy that never ends. You see how imperfect I am, and I cannot deny it in myself. I humble myself before you today; fill me with your grace-filled Spirit that empowers me to live for you.

LONG-SUFFERING LOVE

Over and over Yahweh tested Israel to see if they would faithfully walk in his ways, as their ancestors had done.

JUDGES 2:22

The testing of Israel was less about their lack of perfection in keeping the law and more about the mercy-heart of God. He extended them chance after chance to submit to his leadership. His love would not give up, and it would not let go. The reason why he kept giving them opportunities to turn to him is because he longed for them to know him the way that their ancestors had. He wanted them to experience the power and protection of a people connected to their God through relationship.

Love is patient. How often have we heard that verse from 1 Corinthians 13? It is long-suffering. It never gives up. Love holds out hope. This is the kind of love that Yahweh displayed toward his people, and it is the same kind of love he displays toward us. Through Christ, we can know the unhindered goodness of connection with the Father. We see that he is loving, kind, patient, and generous. May we faithfully follow him, for he is faithful to us.

Faithful Father, thank you for your relentless pursuit of me. I yield to your love and let you have your way in my life. You are so generous in mercy.

LOST ART

He wanted the succeeding generations of Israel,
who had not known war before,
to learn the art of warfare.

JUDGES 3:2

*I*n the passing of generations, we lose the skills that our ancestors once took for granted. The succeeding generations of Israelites did not know what it was like to fight during the Canaanite wars. They had not experienced the power of God rising up on the behalf of Israel to defeat their enemies. They had not learned the discipline of training for battle and partnering with God in claiming their inheritance.

Are there areas of our lives that we have not learned how to fight for because of the times we are living in? Have we lost the art of discipline, of submission, and of cooperation with God in pursuing his promises over our lives? Have we learned what it is to humbly walk with the Lord and partner with his purposes? May we look to the victories of the generations before and prayerfully consider how we can implement values that have been lost.

Wise One, your wisdom spans through lifetimes and generations. It does not grow stale or outdated. I want to live according to your timeless values. Teach me the art of spiritual warfare and holy partnership with your purposes.

TIMES OF TESTING

They remained in the land to test Israel to see if they would obey
Yahweh's commands that Moses had given to their ancestors.

JUDGES 3:4

*W*hen trials and opposition come from every direction, let us not
lose hope or lose heart. The same God who mercifully gives us
victory over our enemies in seasons of fruitfulness is present in the
times of our testing. Will we obey his Word and turn to him? Will
we look to him for wisdom, for help, and for guidance?

There is no situation, no matter how grave, where we are without
the mercy of God. Whenever our faith is tested, let us turn to him.
Even with our questions and doubts, let us wrestle them out with
him rather than let them keep us from engaging with his heart. He
does not dissuade us when we don't know what to believe or how
to trust him. We can submit to his leadership, even without the
confidence we feel we must have. He reveals himself to those who
seek him with all their hearts, so let's never stop pursuing him.

*Yahweh, thank you for being as present in my trials and testing as
you are in my joyous celebrations. You are better than any other
love I've ever known—so faithful and true. I look to you!*

HE ANSWERED

Then the Israelites, with shattered hearts, cried out to Yahweh for mercy, and he answered them by raising up a champion-deliverer to rescue them.

JUDGES 3:9

*W*ith broken hearts in their utter devastation, Israel had nowhere to turn but to Yahweh. They cried out to him for mercy, finally admitting their need for him. And when their repentant cries rang out, the Lord answered them by raising up yet another champion-deliverer.

Sometimes it takes us until we are completely overwhelmed to admit our need for God's help. Oh, that it weren't so! That we would choose to trust him and depend on him before our hearts are broken open in devastating loss. He is mercifully near all who call on him. Our pain is not a punishment. It is an indicator of our need for God's help. May we cry out to God, no matter where we are today. He is ever so near, and he will answer us.

Merciful Lord, I am so grateful that you listen to my cries for help. When I'm in desperate need of you, you do not turn me away. You are my God, and I will look to you through seasons of plenty and depend on you through seasons of turmoil. Be near!

CHAMPION-DELIVERERS

The Spirit of Yahweh was upon him and empowered him to liberate Israel from bondage. He became Israel's champion.

JUDGES 3:10

Othniel was one of many champion-deliverers that Yahweh raised up throughout the time of the judges. Israel's cycles of victory and subsequent wandering reveal our need for our own deliverer. That is where Christ comes into the picture. He stepped up and stepped in as the divine champion-deliverer who, even in death, overcame the power of the grave. He is alive and is our hope, hero, and forever leader.

Christ is the power of God in human form, our liberator from bondage. There will never be someone else like him, and there is no need for another. He is the one who leads us into victory and freedom. He is our wisdom, our strength, and our shield. He is the incarnate example for how we are to live. He is the King of all kingdoms, the Ruler of all creation, and every knee will one day bow at his name. May we yield our lives here and now, living for his kingdom and partnering with his purposes.

Mighty deliverer, you are my champion-deliverer. You lead me out of my bondage and into the promised territory of my inheritance in you. I submit to your leadership, for you are holy, faithful, and true.

YET AGAIN

The Israelites again did what was evil in Yahweh's sight.

JUDGES 3:12

*W*ithout fail, it seems, when the Spirit-led leader of Israel would pass away and some time had elapsed, the Israelites would again stray from walking in the ways of Yahweh and instead assimilate to the ways of the cultures around them. This is human nature. And yet, with Jesus as our living leader, we need never stray far from his ways.

When we have yet again found ourselves wandering back to old patterns and ways of thinking, letting offense override the love that Jesus preached, may we yet again turn to our faithful and present help. There is nothing that his power cannot overcome—no addiction, no cycle of self-protection or harm, no broken mindset. His love overpowers our failures and faults, our wandering ways, and the lies of the enemy. He is better than any other. Yet again, let's come to him. He is the fullness of mercy, and he removes our sins as far as the east is from the west.

Yahweh, you know me well. You know my tendencies and my struggles. When I wander, keep me coming back to you. You are faithful in love, and I never want to be without you.

CRIES FOR MORE MERCY

Then the Israelites, with shattered hearts,
cried out to Yahweh for mercy.

JUDGES 3:15

*E*very broken heart and disappointment is a chance for God to meet us with the generosity of his heart. Even when our pain is caused by our own choices, he does not hesitate to answer our cries when we call out to him. He is so much more consistent in his love than we could ever hope to be. And yet, how often do we wait to cry out to him?

The Lord is merciful and just, and he never refuses a broken and contrite heart. He does not turn us away, no matter how well deserved we may feel that our pain is. He is so much better than we, as humans, are. He does not give up offering grace upon grace to those who look to him for help. He does not grow tired of meeting us with mercy whenever we ask for it, so let's not hold ourselves back from asking.

God of mercy, hear my cries and answer me. You do not censor me, so I will not censor myself before you. You are my only hope! Come to my aid and deliver me again.

July

POWER THROUGH WEAKNESS

Yahweh raised up a champion-deliverer
to rescue them—Ehud, who was left-handed.

JUDGES 3:15

*I*n the Hebrew text, this passage reads that Ehud was "restricted [crippled] in his right hand." No matter what handicap we may have, God will use us. Our weakness becomes our strength, just as Ehud's did.

Let us never disqualify ourselves, or anyone else, based on our weaknesses. God is in the business of using willing people, no matter how healthy or able our bodies are. Every weakness that we have is an opportunity for God to show off his strength in us. He empowers us by his Spirit to display his ability to conquer through our feeble offerings. In truth, Ehud was strong in many ways. But it was his weakness that allowed him to defeat King Eglon. Let us take courage and hope in the fact that God will use the areas where we feel ill-equipped to display his power.

Great God, thank you for using all who submit to you. Display your power through my weakness, Lord. I long to reflect your strength. How creatively wonderful you are to use what we may despise in ourselves to reveal your glory!

LED INTO REVIVAL

When he arrived back in the land, he sounded the war trumpet with a loud blast and rallied the people in the hill country of Ephraim. The Israelites went down from the hills to fight against the Moabites with Ehud leading the charge.

JUDGES 3:27

When we think of the word *revival*, what comes to mind? Is it not a fresh start, a movement toward joy and gladness? That is the meaning in the context of God's presence with us. He is the fullness of our celebration and victory. He is the reason we delight in a fresh movement of his mercy in our lives.

Ehud led the people into their victory, after defeating the king of the Moabites. He led Israel into their triumph. Jesus, in the same way, has disabled the authority of all earthly powers by defeating death. He rallies us and leads us into spiritual battles where he has already claimed the victory. May we follow our triumphant King wherever he leads us, for there is fresh mercy, joy, and the limitless abundance of his life-giving hope.

Jesus, lead me into revival in your presence. Go before me, and I will follow where you lead. You are my victorious King. I worship and celebrate you!

FOLLOW HIS LEAD

"Follow me closely," he said, "and pursue them, for Yahweh
has delivered your enemies, the Moabites, into your hands!"
So they followed his lead.

JUDGES 3:28

*H*ow closely are we following the Lord? Can we hear his voice?
Can we sense the nearness of his presence? Have we done what
he has asked us to do, obeying the directives of his heart? There
are many distractions that can keep us from following the lead of
Jesus. May we lay them down today as we look to where he is.

When Jesus says to move ahead, how do we respond? When
he instructs us to reach out in love to others, do we make a
plan of action and then follow through on it? Let's never stop
pursuing him or pursuing the assignments he has given us. If we
will keep following his lead closely, we will have all we need. He
is a trustworthy leader in this life. He is full of wisdom, solutions,
and tools. He is the worthy One, and he will not lead us into
destruction. He leads us into the abundance of his life and his
everlasting kingdom.

*Jesus, I follow you. I lay aside the distractions that have pulled my
eyes away from you. I will go where you go and do what you say.*

TIMES OF PEACE

On that day, Moab surrendered to Israel,
and the land had peace for eighty years.

JUDGES 3:30

*J*ust as we will most assuredly experience struggles and battles in this life, so we will also have seasons of peace. As we dig into the ground of our victory, where God has planted us, let us tend to the fruit of his divine love, subduing peace, enduring patience, and active kindness.

There is no limit to the bounty of the Spirit's fruit in our lives. In times of peace, where there are no hard battles to be fought, let us focus on tending to the growth of our integrity. Let us remain rooted and grounded in the loyal love of God, letting the gratitude of our hearts toward his generosity compel us to worship and honor him. May we offer him the first fruits of our orchards and vineyards, giving back to him from what he has lavishly given us. May our peace lead us to rejoicing.

Father, thank you for peace in your presence. Keep me tethered to your love, even in times of great calm and in the ordinary pieces of day-to-day life. I'm grateful for your presence at all times.

Raised Up

After Ehud, God raised up Shamgar son of Anath,
who killed six hundred Philistines with nothing but an ox-goad,
and Shamgar the deliverer rescued Israel.

JUDGES 3:31

God raised up Shamgar, son of Anath, as a deliverer. This is extremely significant, for he was not even an Israelite. He was a Canaanite. Yahweh used a foreigner to bring deliverance to the nation of Israel. It does not matter what our lineage is, what our name is, or where we come from. God can use anyone. His presence is more than enough to turn a nobody into a somebody in his kingdom.

May we be careful how we judge others, not based on their outward appearance, because God sees to the heart of a person. He uses the willing and submitted. He uses those who listen to his voice. It does not matter how improbable it seems to us—God does not discriminate! May we reflect his same nature and refuse to discriminate others based on their appearance. Let us remain humble in love and open to the wisdom and leadership of God, no matter what package it may come in.

King of kings, you rule over every nation and have the final say. Instead of being quick to judge, may I be quick in compassion and in humility. Thank you.

A BETTER WAY

After Ehud died, the Israelites returned
to doing evil before the eyes of Yahweh.

JUDGES 4:1

When strong leadership is missing, there is a lack of accountability that runs through the camp. Each goes back to their own way, leading the life that they deem fitting for themselves. It does not take long to adopt destructive habits and prioritize selfish pursuits. Do we resist the wisdom of God, thinking we know better? How often does our pride keep us from responsibility?

The law of the Lord, as we see through Jesus, is the law of love. This includes submission to God and to others, working for the good of society. The law of love directs us to help our neighbors when they are in need, offering shelter when they have none. It takes into consideration what is best, not only for ourselves and our families, but for the greater community. May we choose the better way of Christ's kingdom when faced with the opportunity to break away. He always knows best, and his wisdom is full of consideration and kindness. It is better for us than we know.

Loving Lord, I submit to your law of love and lay aside my rights for selfish gain. I want my life to reflect your principles over my own opinions.

MODERN-DAY DEBORAHS

God raised up Deborah to lead Israel as a champion-deliverer.
She was a prophetess and a fiery woman.

JUDGES 4:4

*I*f we have any questions as to whom God uses in his kingdom,
let us look to the examples in his Word. Deborah is not the
only example of female leadership in the Scriptures, but she is a
profound one. She was fiery and a prophetess. She led Israel into
victorious battles. She acted as a wise counselor and judge.

Let's learn to celebrate the fiery women in our lives. Let's listen
to the wisdom of those who walk closely with the Lord and who
listen to his voice. There is no gender battle in the kingdom of
heaven, and God does not discriminate when it comes to choosing
whom he will use on this earth. Let us be encouragers of the
girls and women who long to make a difference in the world in
significant ways. God uses the willing and humble hearts, and
this is as true for women as it is for men. Let's honor the modern-
day Deborahs in our midst, respecting their God-given gifts and
celebrating their strong personalities.

*Yahweh, I am so thankful that you are an advocate of women.
Teach me how to honor you through my support of them in my
life. Thank you!*

WISDOM GIVER

She presided as Israel's judge under the Palm of Deborah,
a certain palm tree...and the people of Israel came to her
for wise decisions.

JUDGES 4:5

*D*eborah was a wisdom-giver and a prophetic voice to Israel.
She ruled as a prophetess while sitting under the realm of
victory, as symbolized by the palm tree, and received prophetic
revelation. Those who came to her for wisdom received prophetic
declarations and advice to help them decide weighty matters.

Jesus is wisdom personified. He has the solutions to all of our
problems, and he never runs out of revelation to impart to us.
What about other wise people in our lives? Whom do we go to for
advice when we don't know what to do? Wisdom is a treasure. It
is more costly than gold and much more valuable than the finest
diamonds. May we search for it the way we do for hidden treasure.
There are wise ones who listen for the voice of God, and there
is also the Spirit of God with us. Let us open up to the prophetic
declarations of God's perspective over us.

*Wise God, I know that with you are the answers I seek. Speak
to me and give me direction through the wisdom of those who
know and love you.*

CELEBRATE COURAGE

"Very well," she answered. "I will go with you,
but you will receive no glory in the victory
because Yahweh will hand over Sisera to a woman."

JUDGES 4:9

In our fear, when we look for guarantees rather than acting on the courage of faith, there is still victory. Triumph is still on the table, but the glory of the victory may be honored in another. When God speaks to us and we know which way to go and what to do, let's not hesitate to move ahead in confidence. When God promises something, he fulfills it.

May we look to the Lord for courage. May we lean on the encouragement of others, too, when we need it, but let us move ahead into our battlefields with the confidence of what God said that he would do. When we demand a different way, God will still be faithful, but it may not play out as we once anticipated. Even so, let us celebrate the victory. Let us be filled with courage, for the Lord himself goes with us into every battle.

Lord, I want to be quick to respond to your spoken word over my life. As I grow closer to you, may my heart be filled with courage to step out in faith with you.

TODAY'S VICTORY

Deborah prophesied to Barak, "Today, Yahweh has given you victory over Sisera! Go! Yahweh is marching out before you!"

JUDGES 4:14

God is a God of victory. He leads the way into every conflict, marching before us. When we look to him for leadership and direction, we have not only the guarantee of his presence but also of his power with us.

Today, Yahweh has given you victory over the areas where you have felt trapped and hemmed in for far too long. Follow him as he leads you into your triumph. Don't hesitate to confidently press ahead in his presence, for he is giving you the territory that you have been waiting for. May you know the incredible confidence of his faithfulness toward you today as you step out in faith. He is your strong and sure foundation, your Defender, and your help. When he gives you the victory, it is yours to take—but you must march ahead and take it.

Mighty One, I follow where you lead, and I respond to your voice. Guide me into your goodness and into my freedom. I won't shrink back from the battle ahead, knowing you are fighting for and with me. Thank you!

GOD'S HELP

Yahweh threw Sisera and his army into confusion before the onslaught of Barak and his men. Sisera and all his chariots and men were overwhelmed.

JUDGES 4:15

With God's help, what would be impossible on our own becomes possible. When God is with us, nothing can stand against us. He throws armies into confusion and overwhelms them in order to give his people victory.

When God calls us forward in courageous faith, he will make a way for us. He will do what we could not in order to make it possible for us to claim what he has promised. Has he promised you a victory that you just cannot seem to make sense of? Let your confidence be in his ability more than it is in your own understanding. Follow in his footsteps, letting him lead the way. He will never, ever leave you, and he will not abandon you in your struggles. He will not loosen his loving grip on your life. Do what you can and rely on his help for the rest.

Faithful One, I trust you to fight for me in ways that I cannot even fathom. As I move into the unknown, you go before me and work things together for my good. I believe it!

A Woman's Victory

Just then, Barak arrived in pursuit of Sisera.
Jael went out of her tent to greet him and said,
"Come, let me show you the man you're looking for."

JUDGES 4:22

Just as God promised through Deborah, Sisera was overcome and defeated by a woman. Jael did not look like a threat, and yet she was the one who took the enemy down. A woman's victory was the nation's victory. So it is today: a woman's victory is also everyone's victory.

May we not dismiss our own part to play, no matter who we are, what we look like, or what society says that we should or should not do. Our role in the kingdom of heaven, no matter our gender, is important. May we seek after the kingdom of God, looking for ways to faithfully follow through on his Word, never shrinking back in fear.

Yahweh, thank you for your wisdom and power. Thank you for making men and women in your image. Thank you for the part I have to play in your kingdom. Use me, Lord; I am your willing child, and I will serve you and your purposes.

No Holding Back

Deborah and Barak son of Abinoam sang this victory song:
Blessings be to Yahweh, who gave us victory today! For the people
answered the call, and Israel threw off what once held us back.

JUDGES 5:1–2

*I*srael's victory and subsequent celebration is a powerful picture
of our rejoicing in Christ. When we answer the call of God and
we throw off what once held us back, we are able to forge ahead
into the liberty of his love. Christ has overcome the enemies of sin,
death, and captivity. He is our living Redeemer and rescuer.

Let us cast off every restraint that keeps us from moving ahead in
faith. When God speaks, may we respond with willing hearts and
faithful obedience. He is loyal to his word, and he will not let us
down. God does not play tricks on us or change his mind. Let's
take him at his word, knowing that he speaks truth, and his word is
our assurance. No holds barred; let's follow after him.

*Mighty One, when you speak, may my heart be quick to respond.
Spirit, fill me with the courage and confidence of your presence.
I don't want anything to hold me back from your kingdom's
inheritance. I answer your call today.*

MAKE MUSIC

Listen, you kings! Open your ears, you princes! For I will sing a song to Yahweh. I will make music to Yahweh, the God of Israel.

JUDGES 5:3

*M*usic is a powerful connection between our souls and the presence of God. When we play, sing, and dance to the rhythms and melodies of the overflow of our hearts, it transcends our limited vocabulary and language.

Have you ever been moved to tears by a song or performance? Have you ever had to get up out of your seat and dance to the rhythmic music playing around you? Music is more than intellectual, more than emotional, more than physical. It encompasses and involves our whole being. If you are so inclined, make music today. Sing a song, play an instrument, or listen to music that inspires you. As you do, make it an offering to the Lord. Turn your attention to him, even as you let go and let the music move you. Deep calls to deep, and spirit calls to Spirit. Let it out through creative expression today.

Creator, I take time in your presence letting the overflow of my heart lead me in song, in freedom of expression, and in connection to you. I love you!

MOTHERLY CONFIDENCE

Champions were hard to find—hard to find in Israel, until I, Deborah, took a stand! I arose as a mother in Israel!

JUDGES 5:7

Deborah was bold in her faith, and she was unapologetic in her courageous confidence. Just as she arose as a mother to Israel, so let the mothers arise in our spiritual communities! Christ in us is the hope of glory; he is our assurance and resolute strength. There is no reason to shrink into the background waiting to be called out when God has already commissioned us to boldly follow him.

May we let the power of God's Spirit instruct, refine, and build us up in his love. When we have grown in wisdom and in faith, may we rise up and take our places as Spirit-led mothers and fathers who forge ahead into the victory that God has given us. Let us also honor the servant-leadership of those who faithfully show up in the image of Christ's love and truth and heed the wisdom that they impart.

Great God, give me the confidence and boldness of a lion as I walk in your ways. May timidity and fear never keep me from taking the place that you have offered.

EVERYONE DECLARE

Declare it, you rich who ride on your white donkeys, sitting on your fancy saddles! Declare it, you poor who must walk wherever you go!

JUDGES 5:10

Christ's victory is for everyone! May both the rich and poor declare the goodness of God. As Psalm 150:6 pronounces, "Let everyone everywhere join in the crescendo of ecstatic praise to Yahweh!" His loyal love does not leave anyone out. His eternal victory over death is available to people from every tribe and every level of society. It is as accessible to the margins as it is to the mainstream.

Let us celebrate what Christ has done for us. He is so very good, and his love endures forever. May we join in with the chorus of those who sing the praises of God, for he is good to all. He is our victor and our champion. Let everyone, everywhere join in praise to Yahweh and celebrate his goodness. Hallelujah!

Yahweh, I declare your greatness and your goodness. You are so very worthy of my praise, and I will not hold it back. Thank you for your ultimate victory and the freedom I have found in your kingdom.

COMPASSION OVER COMFORT

Among Reuben's clans there was great searching of heart. Gad played it safe and stayed east of the Jordan, and Dan lingered near their ships, while Asher kept their distance and stayed by the coast, safe and secure in their harbors.

JUDGES 5:16–17

*D*o we choose to stay safe and secure in our peaceful harbors when our brothers and sisters are calling out for help? Do we play it safe in the realm of our comfort instead of partnering with those who need our support? When we choose to align with those who need our help, it requires us to move out of our comfort zones. We cannot move in compassion and remain apathetic at the same time.

May we count the cost of our comfort when those around us are shouting rallying cries for justice. Do we love our own lives more than those of our neighbors and friends? Do we value our possessions more than fighting for our brothers and sisters? May we cling to the love of God, letting it challenge where we are placing our own security. When compassion motivates and moves us, it is God's work we are doing.

Compassionate Father, I don't want to love my life more than I do your mercy and justice. May I count the cost of my comfort and follow your compassion instead.

SHINE LIKE THE SUN

Yahweh...may those who love you shine like the sun,
bright in its strength as it crosses the sky!

JUDGES 5:31

Those who love the Lord become like him. When we gaze upon his beauty, it changes us. When we give our time and attention to behold the Lord, we transform into his image. Let us focus on the one thing that truly matters—God with us. Jesus, the hope of glory and the author and finisher of our faith, is the focal point of the gospel. He is our one true Savior, and his ways are better than any other.

When we love something, we prioritize it. We spend as much time as possible with the object of our affection. We compromise and sacrifice our own preferences in order to show them love in ways that are meaningful. May we love the Lord with our whole hearts, souls, minds, and bodies. May we give him time to speak to us, and may we be motivated by his mercy in all that we do. Then we will shine like the sun, bright in its strength.

Light of the World, you are the reason I live and breathe. Fill me with the strength of your love within me and lead me into your glory.

MAN OF COURAGE

Yahweh's Angel suddenly appeared to Gideon and said, "Yahweh's presence goes with you, man of fearless courage!"

JUDGES 6:12

When the Angel of the Lord appeared to Gideon, he prophesied his destiny over him. Gideon would become a fearless warrior. In the same way, God speaks our destinies over us. He often speaks things that are not yet visible and brings them into reality. He calls forth our purpose and intention, and we simply need to follow his lead.

Courage was something that God spoke to his people countless times through the Scriptures. He encouraged them to be strong and courageous, to trust in his help and presence. Courage is not needed when we are in the safety of what we're accustomed to. It is required as we step into the unknown—and life is full of unknowns. We will have opportunity after opportunity to either hesitate or shrink back in fear or to trust what God has said, who he is, and his very presence with us. May we be bold and confident, knowing that no matter what, God is with us.

Lord, speak your truth over my heart and fill me with the courage of your presence. You are the one I look to and depend upon in every moment and in every unknown. I trust you.

EVEN IN INCREDULITY

"Me?" Gideon replied. "But sir, if Yahweh is truly with us,
why have all these troubles come to us?
Where are all his miracle-wonders that our fathers told us about?"

JUDGES 6:13

Gideon did not hold back his earnest questions from the Lord. He did not hesitate to respond and react with honesty. May we do the same. Even when we do not understand, let's be open in dialogue with the Lord and others. Even when our experience defies the stories we have heard of God's greatness, let's not hold back our curiosity. Could this same God who worked miracle-wonders be the same God who is calling us to walk in his power?

Whatever our initial response may be to the Lord's calling over our lives, may we remain open to his voice. May we press in with our questions rather than shoving them down and denying the voice of our Father. There is no need to pretend to understand, but let's wrestle with him in our questioning. Let's move further into honest conversation with God to know his heart and understand his ways.

Yahweh, even when I don't understand, I will not turn from you. I give you the honest reaction of my heart, and I listen for your response. Speak, Lord, and settle my questions with your wisdom.

ALL YOU NEED

Yahweh himself faced Gideon directly and said, "Am I not sending you? With my presence you have all you need. Go in the strength that you now have and rescue Israel from Midian's power!"

JUDGES 6:14

Gideon's divine encounter with Yahweh empowered him to face overwhelming odds and defeat the Midianite armies. The strength he went out in was the strength he gained from this encounter with God, clothed with the power of the Holy Spirit. God himself commissioned Gideon with authority to lead his people into victory.

God's answer to Gideon is the same answer he gives us today, no matter the question. When he sends us, his word is our guarantee of his presence. With his presence, we have all we need. There is nothing more and nothing less that we need to prepare when God says go. Let us follow his lead, knowing that his presence will satisfy the needs we have along the way.

Provider, I trust that when you commission me in your presence, you go with me. I have everything I need right now, and I trust that will be true every step of the way. In faith, I follow you and go in the strength of your presence.

CARRIERS OF GOD'S PRESENCE

"My presence and my power will be with you. Believe me, Gideon,
you will crush the Midianites easily as if they were only one man!"

JUDGES 6:16

With the same words he spoke over Moses when he sent him
to deliver the Israelites from Egypt, the Lord spoke to Gideon.
He promised his presence and power every step of the way. We
know that in Christ, we have unhindered fellowship with the Spirit
of God. He is our sustenance, our strength, and our ever-present
help. He is our peace, our confidant, and our Comforter. God with
us is a forever-promise that will never expire.

May we walk in the confidence of those that have been called
according to the purposes of God and his kingdom. His love draws
us in, and his grace empowers us to follow his kingdom ways. God
will absolutely be with us. Let us remain aware of the connection
we have and look to him whenever our hearts begin to waver. He
is our great confidence, and he will never fail to follow through on
his promises.

*Faithful God, thank you for your presence and power in my life
through your Spirit. I am overwhelmed at your goodness, and I
am undone in the pure mercy of your nearness.*

CONFIRMATION

"If it's really true that you will go with me...
then show me a miracle-sign to prove
that you are really Yahweh speaking with me."

JUDGES 6:17

*G*od is incredibly gracious with us. He is patient in love, and he is willing to meet us where we are. Even after Yahweh had spoken *directly* to Gideon and assured him of his presence and favor, Gideon still wanted more assurance. He wanted confirmation of God's promise that he would go with him into battle.

Don't be discouraged if, when God speaks, you still waver. Gideon pressed in for more assurance, and so can you. It is relationship that God is after, not blind obedience. Relationships are filled with nuance, as well as give and take. If your heart is struggling to trust, be real about it. Press into the presence of God, where he will meet you. He is so merciful toward you. If it's confirmation you desire, pray and ask for it. The Lord answered Gideon, and he will answer you.

Lord, thank you for your patience with me. I long to know you more and to walk in the confidence of your presence. Answer my prayers as I lay them out before you. I look to you.

SUPERNATURAL FIRE

Yahweh's Angel reached out the staff he was holding...
All at once, supernatural fire sprang up from the rock
and burned up the meat and the bread.

JUDGES 6:21

This supernatural fire was the miracle-sign that Gideon was asking for when he requested confirmation of Yahweh's word. He did not know what the sign would be, but the Lord's response was to supernaturally consume the offering he made with fire that appeared from nowhere. Gideon provided the sacrifice, and the Lord himself provided the fire.

When we put our offering on the altar of God, he is the supernatural fire that consumes it. When we lay our lives on the rock of his salvation, he is the burning passion that blazes within. As we readily give him the offering of our faith, he responds with the supernatural power of his presence. The Spirit can be like a fire that refines us, and we become more like him in the process of surrendering to his will.

Refiner, consume the offering of my life and fill me with your holy fire. I want to be so consumed by you that all competing desires burn off until I am one with your love.

BE AT PEACE

Yahweh spoke to him and said,
"Be at peace. Don't be afraid. You will not die."

JUDGES 6:23

When Gideon realized that he had seen the Angel of Yahweh, he was filled with terror. In his understanding, if he saw the Lord face-to-face, the consequence was that he would die, for it was told that no man could see the Lord and live because of the greatness of his glory. Yahweh spoke to Gideon and soothed his fears. "Be at peace," he said. "You will not die."

The Lord did not rebuke his fear, but he spoke assurance to him. When we are afraid, the Lord speaks over us. *Be at peace. Don't be afraid.* He has encouragement for our hearts, and his comfort is near. His words bring light, life, and peace. What he says is always founded in the truth of his character. Let us trust the Lord when he speaks. When he soothes our worried minds, he reassures us of his presence and his peace. "Be at peace. Don't be afraid. You will not die."

Prince of Peace, comfort my worried heart and speak your truth in love. I long to be refreshed in your presence with your right now word. Calm my fears with your comfort.

YAHWEH-SHALOM

Gideon built an altar to Yahweh there
and named it "In Yahweh there is Peace."

JUDGES 6:24

When God breathes peace into our souls with the confidence
of his presence, may we respond by building an altar to him in
our lives. This could be as simple as writing down how grateful
we are for his specific answer to our questions. It could look
like displaying a verse of truth that redirects our focus back to
his presence with us. The possibilities are endless, so we can
be creative in building meaningful memorials that signify our
encounters with God.

The Lord is our Prince of Peace. He is full of shalom that
transcends our understanding. His peace does not erase the
battles we go into; it floods us and keeps our hearts confidently
at rest, even when the battle is raging. Let us take hope in the
persistent clarity of God with us. We do not rely on our own
strength but on his. He is a strong and faithful leader, and he never
leaves us.

*Yahweh, thank you for the shalom of your presence. No matter
what I face, your peace is my plentiful portion. Thank you!*

NOT OUR BATTLE

"If Baal is a god, let him fight his own battles
and defend his own altar!"

JUDGES 6:31

There are many who will fight for a cause that they believe in. How many, though, will let their cause speak for itself? In a world filled with competing interests and powers, may we have the discernment to know when to fight and when to step back and let things play out as they will.

God is always on the side of the vulnerable. He comes to the defense of the innocent and weak. We will find him at the margins where people are suffering. May we keep ourselves from defending powerful people who do not represent the love of Christ. Let's do the work of loving everyone around us, rather than coming under principalities and getting behind those in power who do more to divide and discriminate than encourage unity. May our allegiance lie with Jesus, the King above all kings and the Lord above every lord.

King Jesus, you are my God, and I will follow you. You instructed us to love our enemies and to turn our cheeks when we are struck. I lay down my pride and offense, and I yield to you.

SECRETS OF SUCCESS

The Spirit of Yahweh clothed himself in Gideon
and enveloped him!

JUDGES 6:34

The secret to Gideon's success, and to ours, is in the empowering presence of God. The Spirit of Yahweh fills us when we need a fresh dash of courage to go forth into the fight for our destiny. In all things, in every trial and circumstance, when we ask God for his help, he envelops us in his presence.

The greatest asset we have in our success is our God who is with us. It is his leadership, his power, and his mercy. We face nothing on our own. We need never fear, for God is with us. He is our overpowering strength and the one who propels us into his promises as we partner with his strategies. There is more than enough wisdom, more than enough peace, more than enough grace when we are clothed in Christ. Let's invite the Spirit to envelop our lives.

Spirit, fill me and surround me. Envelop me with your presence and flood my consciousness with your nearness. You are my strength and my courage. In you, I find overcoming victory in every battle. Overwhelm me with your goodness, for I trust in you.

EMPOWERED TO LEAD

Gideon sounded a blast of the shofar
to call the men of the clan of Abiezer to follow him.

JUDGES 6:34

*H*aving been filled with the Spirit of Yahweh, Gideon sounded the battle horn to call the fighters forth. Everyone he called responded. They came to join him in the fight; they followed his confident lead into the battle before them.

When we are empowered by God to lead, people will respond. There is no coercion or manipulation in the leadership of Christ, and there should be none in ours either. When we sound the call, those who are stirred will respond. When we hear the call of others to help them fight their own battles, we, too, will respond in kind. There is empowered leadership, and there is controlled leadership. May we fight for more of the former and leave behind efforts to control others.

Lord, thank you for your empowering presence that moves in mighty ways. I follow you, no matter where it leads me. May I remain submitted to your will and ways all of my life, and may I recognize and support those who do the same.

LAY OUT YOUR FLEECE

"If you have really chosen me...then give me proof. Here—I am placing a wool fleece on the threshing floor"...That night God did what Gideon had asked. The next morning the fleece was dry, but dew covered the ground around it.

JUDGES 6:36, 40

*G*ideon had trouble taking God at his word. Even though Yahweh had revealed himself to Gideon and he had provided supernatural fire to burn up his offering, Gideon still hesitated before the battle. He wanted even more assurance and even more proof of God's promise, not only for himself but also for the men around him. Not only did he lay out one fleece, but he also laid out another the night after and asked God to do the opposite as he had done before.

Each time, God responded and gave Gideon the assurances that he asked for. We may find ourselves questioning, as Gideon did, our calling. Our hearts may wonder whether we truly heard God correctly. When we do, let's not disqualify ourselves and move on. Rather, we can see through God's interaction with Gideon that the Lord is extremely patient with us. When we ask for more reassurance, God gives it.

Yahweh, thank you for being so persistent in kindness. Reassure me with your promised presence and your consistent answers.

UNFAVORABLE ODDS

Yahweh told Gideon, "I will give you victory over the Midianites with the three hundred men who cupped their hands and drank. Tell everyone else to go home."

JUDGES 7:7

*T*hose who cupped their hands to drink from them showed discipline and readiness. Where they were drinking would have been in the sight of the enemy's camp. These disciplined and alert men would become Gideon's army against the Midianites. They were vastly outnumbered—four hundred fifty to one. Those are some unfavorable odds!

God loves to outshine our abilities. He loves to use our weakness to show off his strength. This battle was no different. Though they were outnumbered, Gideon's army was called and chosen by Yahweh. When God calls us, he equips us. He goes before us, and he is with us through the hills and the valleys. Let us continually seek him, listen to his voice, and yield to his leadership. He shines brightest when we are most vulnerable. He takes our discipline and readiness and couples it with his power. What a great God!

Lord, no matter the odds stacked against me, I will follow where you lead. I will obey your voice when you speak. Thank you for your presence that never leaves.

August

GOD'S WISDOM IS BETTER

When Gideon heard about the man's dream and what it meant,
he...worshiped Yahweh. Then he...shouted, "Come on, it's time to
strike! Yahweh is giving you victory over the Midianite army!"

JUDGES 7:15

*T*here are moments in our lives when we are waiting on a signal
to move forward. God does not withhold his guidance from those
who are yielded and ready. Whether it be through a dream, an
opening in opportunity, or the encouragement of those around us,
we will know when it is time to move ahead.

God is infinitely wise, seeing every angle of every situation clearly.
He knows the best timing, so we can lean on his understanding
and leadership more than we do our own anxious impatience.
Let's not rush ahead into something for fear of missing out.
Rather, when we wait for his signal, we can march ahead in the
confidence of his timing. He is with us, and he will not fail to direct
us when we look to him.

*Great God, you are my leader, and I wait on your signal. I trust
your timing. Fill me with courage as I wait on you and as I forge
ahead in my purpose.*

GODLY LEADERSHIP

He told them, "Follow me! When I get to the edge of the camp,
watch me closely and do exactly what I do."

JUDGES 7:17

When we yield our lives to Jesus, we follow his example. We watch him closely and do exactly as he does. This is what Jesus also did; he told his disciples that he only did what he saw the Father doing. He spent time set apart in close fellowship with the Father through prayer, and he submitted to his Father's leadership.

If Jesus did this, how much more should we? We have been given access to the Father through Christ, the Son. We have the Holy Spirit who teaches, corrects, and directs us in the ways of God's kingdom. He is our helper, and he leads us in the example of Jesus. The path of love always makes a way. We simply need to follow Jesus and closely watch him and then do as he does. Let us submit and follow his incomparable leadership.

Jesus, I look to you today and every day. You are the filter that I see my circumstances and relationships through. I choose to follow you and your ways.

HEAVENLY INTERVENTION

When they sounded their three hundred shofars, Yahweh made the enemy troops turn against each other with their own swords.

JUDGES 7:22

When we rely on God's help, he gives it. We do not sit back and wait for him to do it all, but we rely on his partnership in fighting our battles. He is victorious over every enemy we face—over fear, shame, and sin that so easily entangles. He has conquered death and rendered it defenseless against the resurrection power of his love.

As we move ahead into battles that test us, God is with us. As we ready ourselves, God moves on our behalf, and we are able to conquer every enemy with the help of his heavenly intervention. Do not fear the odds stacked against you. When the Lord goes with you, he provides the overwhelming power of his presence to make a way for your overcoming victory. Trust him, for he is faithful and true.

Lord, thank you for going with me into the battles of this life. What overwhelms me does not worry you. I rely on your help, and I am so thankful for the power of your presence at all times.

WOUNDED PRIDE

The men of Ephraim got into a heated argument with Gideon
and complained to him, "Why didn't you tell us you were going
to fight the Midianites? Why did you do that to us?"

JUDGES 8:1

*E*phraim was one of the strongest and largest of the northern
tribes of Israel. They resented that a smaller tribe went into battle
without them near their territory. They were jealous of the victory
that Gideon and his small army achieved, having let their wounded
pride overcome their senses.

When we let our own wounded pride fester, we may become
offended by the triumphs of another. When we watch other, less
qualified people succeed in ways that we are used to succeeding
in, jealousy may cloud our ability to celebrate with them. Let's
remember that the success of another is not a threat to our own.
There is enough room in the kingdom to cheer each other on.
Let's elevate and encourage each other in our accomplishments
rather than letting pride divide us. There is more than enough in
the abundance of God's kingdom for everyone.

*God, thank you that there is abundant victory for us all in your
everlasting kingdom. Here, as I follow you on this earth, may I lay
down my pride and be one who rejoices in the success of others.*

HUMBLE HEARTS

Gideon replied, "What have I accomplished compared to you? What your tribe did is worth so much more than what my whole clan has done...What have I done compared with you?" After he said this, they calmed down and were no longer so angry.

JUDGES 8:2–3

*H*umility keeps us in a place where we can offer compassion to those who are struggling. A humble response to someone else's defensiveness can diffuse an argument. We do not need to play down our own successes when others feel threatened. Though we can, at the same time, encourage and reflect back the truth of another's value and success.

Humility doesn't only benefit the one who offers it, it can also calm the triggered defense of another. Instead of rising to the level of outrage of another, let's practice remaining calm and grounded in the truth of our own experience. Let's cultivate humble hearts, for they will serve us well in this life. If we struggle to know how, let's look to Jesus. He is loving in his leadership and humble in his servanthood.

Humble Jesus, thank you for the example of your humility. May my heart remain calm in your love. When others are offended by my success, help me to speak truth in love.

CONTINUE TO PURSUE

Totally exhausted, Gideon and his three hundred men crossed the river Jordan and continued to pursue the enemy.

JUDGES 8:4

*E*ven in our weariness, we can continue to pursue all that God has for us. If we will not give up, we will experience the ultimate victory that God is leading us into. Though we are weary, let's remember that God has chosen us as his servants. He will not give up, and he will strengthen us along the way.

There are some seasons in this life where rest is fleeting and we are bone-tired. The demands of life can be overwhelming. But if we will not give up hope and continue to pursue the Lord, we will experience his victory. He is our peace, even in our exhaustion. He is our vision, and he will refresh and renew us. Though we may be tired, let us not surrender to hopelessness. He is still working in us, still moving in our lives, and still leading us into triumph.

King Jesus, I will follow you, no matter what. Refresh me in your presence and restore my hope, even in my physical exhaustion. I depend on you, Lord. I will rest when I can and then keep moving forward in faith. You are my pursuit.

MISDIRECTED HOPES

The Israelites said to Gideon, "You're our war hero! You're the one who saved us from the Midianites. You be our ruler!"...
Gideon answered, "No. Neither I nor my son will be your ruler.
Yahweh is to be your only King."

JUDGES 8:22–23

It seems that Gideon had no desire to lead the Israelites after their victory over the Midianites. He did not want to be their king. How often when we see someone overcome incredible odds, do we put them on a pedestal? We praise their courage and their strength, and we look to them for more than we should. In actuality, God in each of us is more than enough. Jesus is to be our King, as Yahweh was to be Israel's only King.

When we put our trust in the capabilities of another more than we do in God, we will inevitably be disappointed. Let us be aware of where we are putting our hope. Who do we look to when things are uncertain? Who do we rely on when we need assurance? Let us look to our God and King first and foremost, for with him, all things are possible.

King of kings, I yield my heart to you and look to you for leadership. I know that you are perfect in all of your ways. I trust you more than any other.

USE WISDOM

"If you have acted honorably and done what is right by Baal-
Fighter and his family today, then may you enjoy Abimelech,
this thornbush king of yours, and may he enjoy you too!
But if not, let fire come out from Abimelech and consume you."

JUDGES 9:19–20

*G*ideon was known in Israel as Baal-Fighter. He led the Israelites
into incredible victory. Though he refused to be king, the Israelites
regarded him as a war hero. Abimelech, one of the seventy sons of
Gideon, thirsted for power and gained it through a murderous plot
to destroy his brothers. The one brother who escaped and lived
rebuked those in Shechem who crowned Abimelech their king.

Corruption is never honored in the kingdom of our God. He
is just, and he rules in wisdom and truth. No wicked plan goes
unseen. May we not fall in line with corruption, thinking that it is a
necessary evil in our world. May we stand on integrity, truth, and
justice. May we live with mercy. Still, may we be careful to never
excuse the corruption of our hearts or our leaders. Let us submit to
God and his wisdom and act honorably.

*Wise One, root out the apathy in my heart that has turned a blind
eye to corruption. Fill me with your love that blazes with mercy,
truth, and justice.*

PRIDE COMES BEFORE A FALL

"If only the people of Shechem were under my command,
then I would get rid of him. I would say to Abimelech,
'Assemble your whole army! We'll defeat them all!'"

JUDGES 9:29

*W*e see later, after all his big talk, that Gaal reluctantly went
out to fight Abimelech. Though he talked big in the beginning,
he did not back it up with the over-confidence he had previously
presented. How much of our pride leads us to say things that we
would never follow through on? Though Gaal did indeed end up
fighting Abimelech, he did so reluctantly and without the self-
confidence his pride had put on at first.

It is important that we learn to remain humble in heart and in
speech. When we spout things that we have no intention of
backing up with action, we open ourselves up to experiences
that may lead to our humiliation. Let us do the work of being
modest with our opinions, especially those that may lead us into
arguments and conflicts with others.

*Lord, I humble myself before you first, and I welcome your
correction in my life. May I stay tethered to your love and mercy
and keep my nose out of business that is not mine.*

DISTINGUISHED BY GOD

Yahweh raised up a man of Issachar's tribe to deliver Israel…
He was Israel's champion-deliverer for twenty-three years.

JUDGES 10:1–2

Graciously, God raises up deliverers whenever his people cry out for help. He is the one who distinguishes leaders and who chooses those who can handle the task. God-appointed leadership is always better than man's choice. The champion-deliverers of Israel were not perfect, but they were yielded to Yahweh's leadership.

May we remain connected to God through hearts of submission. When we allow him to guide us, he will raise us up at the right time. He will use our lives in various ways, with specific purposes to show off the restorative and redemptive power of his mercy. Let us yield to his love, for he will transform us in its life-giving light. In him, there is more than enough room for growth and for overcoming our limitations. As we yield to him, he distinguishes us in the ways that he sees fit. He is truly great.

Jesus, you are the ultimate champion-deliverer. I will follow you anywhere you lead. Use me, mold me, and transform me in your image. Thank you!

THROW YOURSELF ON GOD'S MERCY

The Israelites continued to plead with Yahweh,
"Rescue us! We know we are guilty.
You can do to us whatever seems good to you,
but please, come to our rescue!"

JUDGES 10:15

It is always better to throw ourselves upon God's mercy than it is to be subject to the cruelty of men. He is full of compassion, and he does not deal with us the way that we deserve. Though we stray from his love time and time again, he is always ready to restore us when we return to him. The power of his redemption is made evident as his mercy-miracles meet us in our weakness.

Whenever we realize our guilt and our need for God's help, let us give ourselves over to God, letting him deal with us as he will. We can always know what to expect when we approach him. He is merciful, and he is generous. He helps those who cry out to him. Let us reach out for him every time we are overwhelmed. He is close in Christ, and in the conceding of our hearts, he covers over our guilt and shame. What a wonderful hope we have.

Merciful One, thank you for your love that washes over my guilt. I surrender to your mercy.

GET RID OF BARRIERS

They threw away the false gods from among them
and returned to worshiping Yahweh.
At last, Yahweh felt Israel's misery
and could bear it no longer.

JUDGES 10:16

Though God turns to us every time we turn to him, do we do the work of ridding our hearts and lives of the barriers that keep us from the fullness of his love? When we do not deal with the distractions of idols and the pull of old cycles that we just can't seem to quit, we allow obstacles to remain between the Lord and us.

Let us be relentless in throwing away that which keeps us from pursuing God with our whole hearts. Why would we keep the temptation of these things within our reach when we say that we want freedom in his love? When we dedicate, or rededicate, our lives to Christ, there is a purging that needs to happen at the same time. Anything that stands in the way of true worship and freedom in Christ is a barrier to be dealt with.

Mighty One, I don't want to hold on to anything that keeps me from the power and liberty of your love in my life. Help me to get rid of all the barriers and clear the way for your unhindered mercy.

INTO GOD'S FAMILY

Yahweh raised up a brave, fearless champion from Gilead
to deliver Israel. His name was Jephthah,
and he was the son of a prostitute.

JUDGES 11:1

Jephthah came from the area of Gilead, where he was forced
from his home. The Lord raised him up, though his past was
questionable. God will include even those with social stigmas
in the "honor roll" of faith, as we see in Hebrews. Let us be
encouraged by the extent of God's grace. Everyone gets a place,
and everyone gets to contribute to God's kingdom, no matter the
shadows that they come out of.

May we be fearless in our pursuit of righteousness, and may we
fight the good fight with all of our hearts. No matter where we
come from or what the stories of our pasts are, God's grace is
enough to empower us in his love. He welcomes us into his family
and sets a place for us at his table. When our families reject us, he
never does. He has prepared a place for each of us, so let's take
him up on his offer. He is extravagantly generous in compassion
and completely loving in his acceptance of us as his own.

*Father, thank you for welcoming me into your family and for
covering the shame of my past with your marvelous mercy.*

HUMBLE YOURSELF

Swallowing their pride, they said to him,
"Come and lead us so that we can fight the Ammonites."

JUDGES 11:6

There may be times in life where we realize that our pride led us to drive away those that we actually need. It is never a good idea to push people away because of our stubborn views. When we operate in love and compassion, we will find that pride has no place. Pride pushes people away rather than accepting them. It makes us feel as if we know what's best, and it leaves no room for wisdom's voice.

Even so, when we find ourselves needing the help of others that we pushed away, we can lay down our pride and seek to restore what was lost. If we will take ownership of our faults and admit to our wrongs, we pave the way for restoration. Let us truly have a change of heart, rather than seeking to use others for what they can offer us. God's mercy transforms us, and it teaches us how to humble ourselves in our relationships.

God of wisdom, forgive my selfish pride and my arrogance. Keep me humble in your love as I seek to restore lost connection with others. Thank you for renewing me in your mercy.

PLEDGE OF LOYALTY

"Come and fight the Ammonites. You're the one we need!"
Jephthah said to them, "Very well. If you take me back home to
fight the Ammonites and Yahweh gives me victory, then you will
make me your ruler. Agreed?"

JUDGES 11:8–9

When we make a covenant with others, God is watching. He keeps us accountable. When we pledge loyalty to another, we should never take it lightly. God certainly doesn't. God's word is truth, and it is his vow. We can always take him at his word, for he is faithful to every promise he makes. Even when we stray, his reliability never fails.

Let's look to God and his loyalty when we need reassurance and encouragement. Let us pledge our loyalty to him. He will not fail us—not even in helping us remain true to him. His mercy is fresh and new in every moment, empowering us by the grace of his presence. He helps us to choose what is right when we lean on him. He never disappoints in his love, and he leads us into the generosity of his kingdom. Let's follow his ways.

Faithful One, thank you for your unfailing promises. I know that you are true, and you will do what you said. Help me to be a person of my word as well.

TRY TO UNDERSTAND

Jephthah sent messengers to the king of Ammon to ask,
"What is your quarrel with us?
Why have you invaded our country?"

JUDGES 11:12

Instead of sending out an army to attack the Ammonites,
Jephthah gave the king an opportunity to explain his quarrel.
Jephthah sought to understand the reasoning of the invasion of
his land. This is like him offering an olive branch by giving the
aggressor the opportunity to reconsider their actions. What a
picture of wise leadership.

When an attack against us is imminent, are we quick to retaliate or
defend? Or, when we have the warning signs and the opportunity,
do we first seek to understand and diffuse the situation? God is
always giving us chances to turn from our ways. Do we do the
same for others? May we be people who emulate the mercy of
God in reaching out in curiosity and with an open heart to come
to a settlement before conflict erupts.

*Merciful One, I follow your loving lead in calm and in chaotic
situations. I trust that your wisdom works in all circumstances.
Help me to seek to understand others, even as you offer me the
understanding of your heart.*

HISTORY LESSON

"Israel seized neither the land of Moab nor the land of Ammon.
When the Israelites left Egypt, they passed through the desert to
the Red Sea and came to Kadesh."

JUDGES 11:15–16

History can instruct us, though it may not sway those who are biased to believe what they will. The offense of a generation can be passed down through families and territories. May we be willing to look at the history of our communities and nations through the lens of truth and not simply through the conditioning of our families and regions. May we be open to humbly hearing the perspectives of others.

With hearts that seek to understand and to come to an agreement without fighting, we make peace possible. When we are humble in our offerings of truth, we don't need to yell or overpower the voice of another. Wisdom has no need to shout. Let us be grounded in the truth of God's kingdom ways and in his Word without picking fights with those who don't see things the same way.

Wise One, thank you for your truth that stands firm, no matter what we believe or don't believe. I align my heart with you and your mercy.

LET YAHWEH BE THE JUDGE

"No, I have not wronged you; rather, you are doing me wrong by attacking me. Let Yahweh be the judge, and let him decide today which of us is right, Israel or Ammon."

JUDGES 11:27

Are we quick to rush to our own defense, or do we let God be the judge and our Advocate? He is the one who knows absolute right from wrong; he sees every intention of each heart laid out clearly before him. When our bargaining leads nowhere, we have nothing to do but leave it in God's hands. If we must fight a battle, we can do it knowing that we did our best to prevent it.

When we know that we have not wronged another, it does not mean that there is no action to be taken if they won't back down. We must lean into the wisdom of God and do what we know to do. God is the only judge, so let us not resort to fighting in a way that dishonors another. Let's lean on the Lord's defense and follow him into the battle with confidence in his sovereignty.

All-knowing One, you know the intent of every heart, and you don't miss a thing. I trust your advocacy and your mercy. I let you be the judge, no matter what.

EMPOWERED BY GOD

The Spirit of Yahweh rushed upon Jephthah and empowered him.
He and his men marched through Gilead and Manasseh
and returned to Mizpah in Gilead.

JUDGES 11:29

Whenever we submit to God before we go into any conflict,
God empowers us with his presence. We can confidently go
ahead into our day with the knowledge that God is with us.
When we yield to his leadership, he is the one who guides us—the
frontrunner of our faith.

No matter what you are facing today, look to the Lord for help.
His spirit-strength is available to you through the fellowship of his
Spirit. He is with you, here and now, closer than your very breath.
He is the courage that rises within your soul. He is the resolute
confidence that fills your mind. He is the energy that rushes
through your body and readies you for what is ahead. Go forth in
the power of his presence.

*Spirit, you are my sustenance and strength. Fill me with your
power, wisdom, and clarity. Lead me in your might. I depend on
you more than I rely on anything else. You are my help, and you
are my victory.*

HALL OF FAITH

Jephthah crossed the river with his men to fight the Ammonites, and Yahweh gave him victory.

JUDGES 11:32

When we follow the Lord and depend on his help for our victory, we are acting in faith. When we take God at his word, and we offer him the trust of our hearts, our confidence does not lie in our own abilities; rather, it rests in the overwhelming mercy-strength of God.

Our journey in life is not one endless battlefield, though we will have moments where we need to fight for our inheritance. We are not required to battle at all times. When fights present themselves and we cannot avoid them, the Lord rises up on our behalf and leads the way into our triumph. He is the one who comes through for the vulnerable. He uses our strength as well as our weakness and amplifies them with the power of his might. He is able to do immeasurably more than we could ask or imagine, so let's rise up in the confidence of his character and let faith in his faithfulness be our rallying cry.

Yahweh, you are the one who holds my victory. I trust you and your unfailing love to never leave me in my battles. Help me to overcome by the blood of the Lamb. Thank you!

WILLING SURRENDER

She said to him, "My father, you have made a vow to Yahweh
and he has delivered you from your enemies, the Ammonites.
Do to me what you promised him you would do."

JUDGES 11:36

*J*esus willingly became the sacrifice for us all, and it is through
him that we find the abundance of life. Every debt we owed was,
and is, satisfied in the blood of Jesus. There is no more for us to
add to his holy offering. We readily give him the reins of our lives,
for he is the Overcomer and the perfect Lamb. In his resurrection
power, the claim of sin and death over us was broken, and we are
made new in him.

Let us willingly surrender to the ways of his kingdom, recognizing
the superiority of his wisdom over our own. Let's wrestle through
our questions with him, not apart from him. He has all the
clarity we are searching for, and his perspective expands our
understanding. Let's lean into the presence of God for the answers
we need. May our vow be to honor him, to submit to him, and to
follow him all the days of our lives.

*Wise God, I surrender to your kingdom and its ways. I align
my life with your heart, and I stand in the confidence of your
resurrection power making all things new in my life.*

LAY DOWN OFFENSE

Jephthah's actions grievously offended the men of Ephraim. They assembled their forces...to confront Jephthah..."Why did you cross the border to fight the Ammonites without inviting us to join you?"

JUDGES 12:1

*T*he men of Ephraim were "grievously offended" by the fact that Jephthah went into battle without them. They let the offense of their hearts turn to violence, throwing insults at the men of Gilead. The result of this was their utter defeat.

Offense can lead us to pick fights that we are not suited to win. Why would we create conflict with our brothers and sisters when the Lord is moving in their lives? Why should we dictate what the favor of the Lord looks like? When we let jealousy override our reasoning and we let spite take the place of love, we are the ones who will suffer. Instead, when we recognize the tendrils of bitterness rising within us, let us take it to the Lord and lay it down. His law of love will never fail, and we will be softened in the presence of compassion.

Mighty God, may I remain in your compassion, not picking fights with those who are doing what you have called them to do. You are better than I am, and your love melts away my offense and brings clarity to my emotions.

FAITHFUL TO PROVIDE

After Jephthah, Yahweh raised up Ibzan,
a champion-deliverer from Bethlehem who ruled Israel.

JUDGES 12:8

Ibzan was the ninth champion-deliverer and came from the tribe of Zebulun. God was faithful to provide deliverer after deliverer to lead Israel. He never failed to raise up men and women who listened to his voice and followed his direction.

God is still faithful to provide, and we can be a part of his plan of deliverance through our submission to his leadership. Jesus is the ultimate deliverer. He is alive, and his place will never be taken, for he is our living hope and our eternal Savior. As we surrender to his guidance, following his loving lead through close fellowship with his Spirit, we will experience the abundance of his life within us. The companionship of Holy Spirit is available to all of us in the same measure. There is nothing that separates us from the love of God in Christ, so let's hold nothing back from him today. Let's run into the open arms of our loving Father, who has all that we need.

Faithful Father, I come to you with a humble, hungry heart. Fill me with your Spirit and speak to me. Teach me your ways, and I will walk in them. I love you!

MIRACLE CHILD

The Angel of Yahweh appeared to her and said,
"Look here! You are no longer barren and childless,
for you will conceive and give birth to a son."

JUDGES 13:3

*M*any women throughout the Old and New Testament encountered God. Angels appeared to more than one woman announcing the supernatural healing of their wombs. They were told that they would conceive and have a child. Often, when this is mentioned in Scripture, the life of the child is then also illuminated. The child of Manoah and his wife, as described here in this passage, would grow up to be the famed Samson.

The Lord often moves in mysterious ways, bringing life out of the ashes of our disappointment. Is there a hope that you have that you are ready to give up on? Ask God to breathe on it. Ask him to speak to you and to move in powerfully mysterious ways to bring redemption and power into the story of your frustration. He is a miracle worker, and he loves you.

Mysterious One, I don't claim to know how you will move in my life, but I give you the longings of my heart. Breathe hope in areas that are desperate for your life-giving touch.

DEDICATED TO GOD

"You will conceive and will give birth to a son. Raise the boy as one dedicated to God from the womb and never cut his hair. He will begin to deliver Israel from Philistine power."

JUDGES 13:5

God's instruction to Samson's parents was that they were to raise their son as a Nazarite. This meant that he would be dedicated to God from birth. Nazarites were forbidden to cut their hair, drink alcohol, or touch anything that was dead. Samson would be raised consecrated to the Lord and set apart for his purposes.

What does it look like for us to dedicate our lives to God? Christ is the Holy One, and it is in the cleansing power of his blood that we are made new. We are consecrated to God in the offering of our hearts and lives to him. There is no prescriptive answer to this question of dedication, though the heart posture is always the same. May we go to the Lord and seek his wisdom for how to live our lives. As we dedicate ourselves, and our households, to the Lord, he will use us for his plans of redemption and restoration.

Holy One, I dedicate my life and my family to you. Guide me in your wisdom and fill me with the assurance of your presence.

SHARE GOOD NEWS

Manoah's wife went to her husband and said, "A man sent from God came to me!...he told me, 'You will become pregnant, and you will have a son...the boy will be fully devoted to God.'"

JUDGES 13:6–7

Good news is meant to be shared. When we are given a good report, who is the first person we tell? Often, it will be those closest to us. A shared joy multiplies our delight. May we not hold back good news with those who have also shared in our struggles. Our rejoicing may also become their reason to celebrate.

This is not to say that discernment does not play a role in our sharing of wonderful news. Manoah's wife shared the news with her husband, but she did not shout it to the village where they lived. Use the discernment of the Spirit to know when to be open and when to hide it in your heart. In due time, your celebration will be evident for all, but don't feel the pressure to rush into telling everyone. Just as we share in our struggles with a select few, we should also be intentional about whom we share our breakthroughs with.

Wonderful God, thank you for your breakthrough power. What a delight it is to rejoice in breakthrough with those who know me well. I'm so grateful!

Prayer for Wisdom

Manoah pleaded with Yahweh, "O my Lord, please send the man of God back to us. Have him come to instruct us how to raise the son who is to be born."

JUDGES 13:8

*G*od is a God of details. He has all the wisdom that we need. Do we struggle to find our way in our limited understanding, or do we press into the Lord for more wisdom, more discernment, and more instruction? He never turns a cold shoulder or ignores our cries for help when we call out. He is more than willing to share his perspective with us and to guide us with his unmatched wisdom.

Whatever it is that we need help understanding, the Lord knows. He always has heavenly solutions for our earthly problems. He has the best answers for our most difficult questions. His wisdom brings clarity where the fog of confusion has set in. May we pray to God and wait on his help when we need it. He gives direction through a variety of ways, and we know his voice by the fruit of his Spirit in our lives.

Spirit of Wisdom, I need your direction, your solutions, and your help. I rely on you. Thank you for fellowship, where I can know you Spirit to spirit. Speak to me. I am listening!

PURPOSE IN LIFE

Manoah replied, "Well, when Yahweh fulfills your prophecy,
how should we raise the boy, and what is his life mission?"

JUDGES 13:12

*P*rayer is a wonderful place to explore our questions. It is more a conversation than a monologue. Just as Manoah asked the Angel of Yahweh for direction in how to raise their miracle child, we, too, can present our curiosity to the Lord through prayer. Jesus told us that if we ask anything in his name, we would have it. What answers are you looking for? What questions are rolling around in your mind that you have yet to ask the Lord?

Have you ever considered that God can use you in specific ways for the glory of his kingdom? Do you have vision for your life? God has a mission for each of us, so let's press in to know what that unique mission is. Perhaps it is like the great river of God's grace, wide and flowing freely to the ocean of his loving-kindness. If the aim of your life is to love well, that is a beautiful mission. If it is to advocate for the vulnerable, that is a marvelous reflection of God's mercy. Whatever the vision, may it serve to propel you and to keep you in his presence.

Wonderful One, thank you for my purpose in you. Lead me on.

WONDER-WORKING GOD

Manoah prepared the young goat and his grain offering
and took them to the rock to offer them up to Yahweh,
the wonder-working God.

JUDGES 13:19

*N*early every time a person in the Old Testament encountered the Angel of Yahweh, their response was to offer a sacrifice. When Manoah took his offering to the rock altar, he did it as a sign to the Lord that he was grateful for the answers to his prayer. God had responded to Manoah's request for more direction from the Angel, and he was grateful for it.

Our God is still a wonder-working God today. He has not changed from answering the prayers of his people. When we request wisdom, he freely gives it. When we ask for help, he provides it. Let us respond to his generosity with sacrifices of praise. Let us offer him true worship from overflowing hearts of gratitude. How wonderful he is, and how faithfully he comes through for us time after time.

Wonderful One, thank you for answering my prayers and for your persistent presence. I offer you my unhindered praise today, for you have been so good to me. Here is the sacrifice of my worship. Burn it up in the fire of your presence.

VISITED BY GOD

Only then did Manoah realize that he
had met the Angel of Yahweh!

JUDGES 13:21

The Angel of Yahweh was God in the form of a human. This is evident in the description Manoah's wife gave as a "man sent from God." The incomprehensible God, the unknowable One, revealed himself to Manoah and his wife. They saw the Lord, and yet they lived to tell the story. The Angel of Yahweh was wrapped in the flames of the fire that burned up their offering and ascended into the sky.

Could you imagine such a sight? What a glory-filled encounter! God himself answered their cries for direction. He spoke to them face-to-face and delivered the guidance they had asked for. God, through his Spirit, does the same with us today. Though he speaks through many different channels and avenues, he also speaks directly to our hearts through his Spirit that is alive in us. His words impart life, truth, clarity, and hopeful expectation. May we learn to recognize him when he encounters us by the fruit of his words and the glory of his presence with us.

Glorious One, there is no one else like you. Thank you for choosing to encounter your people and answer their questions. Meet with me now with the power of your presence. I am expectant.

YAHWEH'S BLESSING

Manoah's wife gave birth to a son, and she named him Samson.
The boy grew up with Yahweh's blessing on his life.

JUDGES 13:24

When we dedicate our lives, as well as the lives of our children, to the Lord, we receive and impart the blessing of God. Yahweh's blessing covers and guards us. His presence goes with us wherever we go. We are washed in the mercy of his kingdom, and he turns our faith-filled steps into paths of his faithfulness.

Proverbs 10:22 states: "True enrichment comes from the blessing of the Lord, with rest and contentment in knowing that it all comes from him." There is no labor or sorrow attached to the knowledge that God provides all we need. We rely on him for every provision along the journey of this life. He is our source and our supply, and we are enriched by his incredible miracle-mercy in our lives.

Yahweh, my life is submitted to you, dedicated to your kingdom ways. I want to walk in the confidence of your mercy all the days of my life. Keep me close to your heart as I follow you through the hills and valleys of this life.

September

HEART STIRRED

The Spirit of Yahweh began to stir his heart
while he was between Zorah and Eshtaol, in the Camp of Dan.

JUDGES 13:25

When God stirs our hearts, it is like a bell being struck within us. He rings the chime of our spirit, alerting us to his presence. His work within us makes a striking difference. When he pulls us in a direction, we sense his leadership. When the Spirit of Yahweh began to stir in Samson's heart, he was in a narrow pass, seemingly between a rock and a hard place.

Is that not the case with us? When we are in situations where we do not see a way out or a probable solution, God stirs within our hearts. He provides the pull that we need to follow him. When our lives are dedicated to God and to his purposes, we need never question his presence. His leadership is sure, and he will make himself known to us and within us at the right time. Let's keep moving in his love, trusting his guidance will be there when we need it.

Spirit, stir my heart in your presence today. I want to know you more, to be drawn into your love, and to rise in the confidence of your faithfulness. I trust you.

PART OF THE PLAN

His parents had no idea that Samson's passion for the girl was part of Yahweh's plan to create an opportunity to come against the Philistines who ruled over Israel at that time.

JUDGES 14:4

How often have we looked at someone else's decision and thought that they were off base? Though we may not have chosen the same path, it does not mean that God is not in it. Samson's choice of a wife was not who his parents expected. They wanted him to find a wife from their own tribe. Yet it was Samson's choice that God would use to further his destiny.

We can trust God to use the choices we make, as well as those of others, to further his kingdom in our lives and in the world. He can use anything. His mercy is large enough to move through our choices and bring about redemption. He is so very good, and we cannot mess up his plan. It is larger than us, and it is more gracious than our understanding.

Sovereign God, I'm so grateful that you use my choices to bring about your purposes, even in unexpected ways. Move through my life and continue to weave your mercy-thread through my story.

PROTECTED AND EMPOWERED

The Spirit of Yahweh entered Samson and empowered him to tear the lion to pieces with his bare hands as if it were a young goat!

JUDGES 14:6

In a moment of danger, where a full-grown lion came roaring toward him, the Spirit of Yahweh rushed upon Samson and empowered him to overcome the lion's strength with supernatural vigor. In that moment, the Spirit of God both protected and strengthened him.

Nothing can stop God's calling over our lives. When we are submitted to him, his Spirit rushes upon us in times of great need to shield and to empower us. We need never fear the dangers of this life when we are walking in the light of God's love. He is our armor and our defense. He is the one who strengthens us in our weakness and emboldens us in our purpose. May we walk in the confidence of his nearness, his wisdom, and his protection. Let us keep moving in courage as he leads us on the path of our destiny.

God, you are my safe place and my courage. You give me strength for my weakness and power for my battles. I trust your faithful provision as I follow you.

JUSTICE IS THE LORD'S

The Philistines replied, "We've come to capture Samson
and repay him for what he did to us."...Samson replied,
"I only did to them what they did to me."

JUDGES 15:10–11

*I*n a world where vengeance seeks its recompense, there is no end to the potential of violence that could play out. In Christ, all vengeance was put to death. Jesus clearly showed us a better way to live. Romans 12:19 instructs that we not be "obsessed with taking revenge, but leave that to God's righteous justice." Only his justice will satisfy.

Jesus spoke to his followers about vengeance, saying in Matthew 5:38–39, "Your ancestors have also been taught, 'Take an eye in exchange for an eye'...However, I say to you, don't repay an evil act with another evil act." Before we justify our need for revenge, let's remember that justice is not ours but the Lord's. The instructions of Jesus are clear: to love our enemies and to offer mercy instead of retaliation.

Righteous One, thank you for the law of your love that is better than the laws of this world. Help me to extend kindness instead of hatred and mercy instead of revenge. I know this is your way.

FAITHFUL TO ANSWER

God answered Samson's prayer and split open
the rock basin under Lehi, and water gushed out!
Samson drank and his spirit was revived.

JUDGES 15:19

As we have already seen time and time again, God answers those who cry out to him for help. He is near to the brokenhearted, and he is close to the vulnerable. He does not despise our weakness. He delights in strengthening us in his comfort. When we need him, he faithfully responds. He is loyal to those who look to him.

May we never hold back our prayers from the Lord. He knows what we need, even before we ask it. He loves to astonish us with his goodness. He knows how quickly we forget his kindness, and he graciously shows up in compassionate truth whenever we need it. Our prayers don't need to be perfect for him to answer. He always answers, no matter how desperate or how discouraged we may feel in our crying out to him for help. He is faithful, and he will always come through.

Faithful One, thank you for your incredible and loyal love. I'm grateful that you accept me as I am and listen to my heartfelt prayers. Meet me in the midst of my mess today.

SPRINGS OF COMFORT

He named that place,
"The Spring for the One Who Cried,"
and it is still there in Lehi to this day.

JUDGES 15:19

God answered Samson's cry by opening up a rock, causing water to gush out. Samson drank, and his spirit was revived. God has reserved a hidden spring for those who cry. When you find yourself weighed down by sorrow, there is a place where you can find refreshment for your soul. If grief has broken open your heart and tears have covered your face, know that there is a spring of restoration that God has for you.

Drink deeply of the living spring of his presence, and he will comfort you and restore you. There is redemptive power in the refreshing of your soul. You don't need to try harder to get past your grief. Cry out to God in the midst of it, and he will meet you there. He will reply to your sobs with his peace-filled presence. His power will revive and restore you in the springs of his comfort.

Comforter, meet me in the depths of my pain and restore my heart in the living springs of your presence. I rely on you, Lord. There is no one else who can revive my weary heart the way that you do.

SUPERNATURAL STRENGTH

On his way out of Gaza, he took hold of the doors of the town gate and ripped them off their hinges...He hoisted them all on his shoulders and carried them off a great distance.

JUDGES 16:3

The supernatural strength that filled Samson helped him to accomplish what seemed impossible. He tore down the city gates and carried their heavy weight nearly forty miles from where the city stood. These were not some garden gates either. They probably stood at two stories high, and he also carried with him the heavy posts that secured the gates. This was a superhuman feat.

In Christ, we can do all things. His strength becomes our own, and he empowers us with his might. Though we may be weak in our own abilities, Christ's power is more than enough to strengthen us to do the impossible in his name. As Ephesians 3:20 says, may we "never doubt God's mighty power to work" in us and accomplish all that he has called us to, "for his miraculous power constantly energizes [us]"!

Jesus Christ, you are my strength. Your resurrection power takes my feeble offerings and does far more in my life than I could ever do on my own. Thank you!

CONVINCED TO CONFESS

Finally, he confessed to her everything: "I've never had my hair cut,
because my parents dedicated me to God from birth.
If anyone cuts my hair, my power will leave me."

JUDGES 16:17

*H*ave you ever been convinced to share a secret that you had
held close to your heart? Have you ever been worn down by the
efforts of others to compromise your integrity? We must be on our
guard and let discernment play a role in our relationships. Delilah
was untrustworthy, and this was proven time and again when she
would try to entrap Samson before this moment. Why, we might
think, would Samson trust her at all?

We must be wise with those we let close to us. Their influence
is unmistakable. If we continually choose to let others who
have proven their lack of integrity influence our lives, then the
consequences we face should not be a surprise. Instead, let's be
discerning with our friends and close confidants. Let's surround
ourselves with those who are honest and who want the best for
us—not those who use us for their own gain, as Delilah did.

*Merciful One, thank you for the clarity of your wisdom. Give me
strength to choose my confidants with integrity and discernment.
I don't want to leave room for unhealthy compromise in my life.*

COMPROMISE WEAKENS

When Delilah realized he had finally disclosed his secret,
she sent for the Philistine rulers.
"Come quickly!...He's finally told me his secret!"

JUDGES 16:18

*T*he lack of discernment in Samson's relationship with Delilah
led to the compromising of his strength. She let the lure of bribes
corrupt her heart and looked for ways to make Samson vulnerable
to capture. When he finally revealed the truth of his strength,
Delilah took advantage and cut his hair. Then she called for the
Philistine rulers to come and take him away.

In her deceit, Delilah schemed against Samson. Delilah cannot be
solely blamed, for Samson allowed this to happen by continuing
to let her close to him when she had already proven to be
untrustworthy. He kept going back to her, perhaps letting pride
fool him into thinking he was indestructible. But our compromising
of our values undermines the strength of our integrity. May we
remain close in Christ, discerning what does not serve us well in
relationships. May we choose our close companions wisely, and
may we humbly remember that we are but dust and that we need
the Lord and his mercy.

*Lord, you are uncompromising in your mighty mercy. I want to
walk so closely with you that I choose your ways over my own. I
depend on you.*

JUST ONCE MORE

Then Samson prayed to Yahweh,
"Lord Yahweh, please remember me again.
O God, impart your strength to me just one more time."

JUDGES 16:28

The Lord in his mercy offers us opportunities for redemption and restoration. Samson knew that he had messed up, but in his captivity, he asked for the Lord's strength to come back to him one more time. How often have we depleted our resources and chosen ways that lead to our captivity? Even there, we can cry out to God for his help.

God's mercy meets us where we are and enables us to do the impossible by the empowerment of his Spirit within us. No matter what choices we made to get to where we are, the grace of God still answers our cries. Do not be discouraged if you find yourself in a mess of your own making. Even there, God can use you. His mercy can turn your shame into a place of healing. Cry out to him, for he is always ready to answer you.

Almighty Yahweh, thank you for your mercy that is far beyond my understanding. I cry out to you today. Answer me by your Spirit.

WHATEVER THEY WANTED

In those days, Israel had no king.
People did whatever they wanted to do.

JUDGES 17:6

*W*ithout clear leadership, people do whatever they want. When there is no vision for a people, a group, or a family, each member follows his or her own way. Are we submitted to the Lord's leadership in our lives? He is our rightful King, and he has given us his wisdom to lead us through the twists and turns of life. We have his Word, and we have his fellowship through his Spirit. There is no reason for us to go it alone in any area of life.

When our lives are built upon the foundation of Christ and his leadership, our choices will show it. When we choose to extend mercy to others instead of building walls of hostility, we reflect his love in our lives. When we choose to bless those who curse us instead of trying to take them down, we show that we belong to him. Instead of doing whatever we want, let's do what he has taught, and still teaches, us to do.

King Jesus, I yield my heart and life to you. Lead me in your love and teach me the wisdom of your ways so that your mercy is reflected in my choices.

FALSE CONFIDENCE

> Micah declared, "Now I know that Yahweh will bless me
> and prosper me, since a Levite now serves as my priest."
>
> JUDGES 17:13

It is right and necessary to depend on others for wisdom and support in life. That is not, however, what Micah was doing here. He was looking to be blessed by the Lord without submitting to him. He wanted to prosper without sacrificing anything of true value to himself. He wanted to use a priest from God's people to ensure his own prosperity. Instead of displaying humility before the God of Israel, Micah acted in self-serving pride.

Our confidence does not come with our affiliations. Those we surround ourselves with cannot be a substitute for the necessary building of relationship with the Lord one-on-one. When we place our confidence in life, let alone our confidence in Christ, on those we associate with rather than on the Lord himself, we will inevitably falter. Let's instead go to our great High Priest, Jesus, who is our true confidence and strength.

Jesus, I don't want to neglect my relationship with you, thinking I have a better chance at fulfillment in others. You are the only one who truly satisfies, and you are the way, the truth, and the life.

RECOGNIZED

They recognized the voice of the young Levite, so they went over to him and asked, "Why are you here? Who brought you here? What are you doing in this place?"

JUDGES 18:3

*H*ave you ever been somewhere far from home and instantly recognized a familiar accent? The pull of the recognizable in such a foreign place may cause you to search the person out. Questions ensue. You may ask them where exactly they are from and how they came to be there. It was this kind of situation that the Israelite men experienced when they overheard the young Levite in an unexpected place.

No matter where you roam on this earth, you will find that the world is smaller than you expected. You will encounter the familiar in the oddest places. You will meet others with whom you somehow already have a connection. It is one of the most wonderful experiences. You can be sure today that, no matter where you go, the Spirit of God is with you. He is your familiarity and your home. Rest in his presence, knowing that you are seen and known by the King of kings.

Lord, thank you for being my home. My heart recognizes your voice, and I know you recognize mine. It is a delight to be yours.

EYES OF YAHWEH

The priest replied, "You have nothing to worry about. The eyes of
Yahweh are watching over your mission. You will succeed."

JUDGES 18:6

The eyes of Yahweh go before you into your day. He sees
everything before it happens. He will go with you, leading you
through the obstacles as you look to him. He will give you wisdom
and discernment to avoid the traps laid out to ensnare you. He will
give you the patience and strength you need to wait on his timing
when he instructs you to do so. Let your heart grow in even more
confident trust in your divine warrior-chief.

Do you want to know if your mission will succeed? Go to Jesus,
who is your great High Priest and ask for his perspective. Align
your heart with his in humble submission and let his Spirit guide
you in truth. Do not hastily push ahead without consideration and
planning. Let the Lord advise you, observe his instruction, and then
you will succeed.

*Yahweh, look over what lies ahead of me and prepare me. Lead
me in your love as I submit to your guidance. I trust you!*

PURSUED AND PERSUADED

The Levite set out with his servant and a pair of donkeys
to find her, win back her heart, and try to persuade her
to return home with him.

JUDGES 19:3

The faithful love of God pursues us even when we are unfaithful to him. This picture of the Levite pursuing his lover in order to woo and win her back is reminiscent of the story of Hosea. Hosea kept patiently pursuing his wife every time she was unfaithful to him. This is also a beautiful picture of how God lovingly and faithfully pursues us.

The kindness of the Lord leads us to repentance. It is his gentleness that draws us to his heart over and over again. He reminds us of the way he sees us, the purity with which he loves us, and how much we mean to him. These are not empty words to control us. They are his pure passion. He is so very patient with us, and his persuasion is lined with love. When presented with such lavish love, how could we turn away?

Jesus, your love is more beautiful and pure than any other I have known. There are no strings attached and no shadow of shame or blame hiding in your heart. Thank you. How I love you!

HOLY HOSPITALITY

"Rest easy," said the old man. "I'll take care of all your needs.
You won't need to spend the night in the square."
So the old man took them into his house.

JUDGES 19:20–21

When we notice others without a place to stay or food to eat, how do we treat them? Do we pretend to not see them, or do we blatantly ignore them? Or does compassion move us to buy them a meal or, even more generously, to open our home? There are as many ways to show hospitality as there are people in this world. When we offer relief to another, welcoming them in the name of the Lord, we offer the same kind of reception they get in Jesus' love.

If we want to reflect the love of God in our lives, hospitality will play a part. We can be creative with what this looks like. We don't need to find a cookie-cutter way to do it. Let's spend time with the Lord, asking him to show us how we can authentically show up in welcoming ways to relieve the worries of another when they are in need. Let's offer the kind of love that does not expect anything in return—only to bless another.

Jesus, I want to be open and hospitable to others. I will partner with you in welcoming them. Teach me.

HOLY OUTRAGE

All the people stood in unison and declared,
"None of us will go back to our cities or return to our homes."

JUDGES 20:8

*T*he outrage the Israelites felt when they heard about a horrible atrocity committed against one of their own caused them to band together to demand justice. They could not ignore the awful act, and they could not simply go back to their ordinary lives without asserting themselves in some way.

When we hear about injustices in this world, what is our reaction? When it hits close to home, it may move us more readily than when it feels far away. We have all witnessed communities coming together to cry out for justice in our lifetime. This is not a new phenomenon. When there are people who are targeted, oppressed, and victimized, they will rise up in unison. They will refuse to go back to normal until the right is wronged. Can we mourn with those who mourn in these times? Can we offer peace to those who are raging? May we be those who are moved by compassion, not shrinking back in apathy or defensively antagonizing the grieving.

Lord, may I never turn a blind eye from the holy outrage against injustice. Give me a heart that rises up with those crying out for your justice.

UPHOLD JUSTICE

But the Benjamites refused to yield
to the demands of their brothers the Israelites.

JUDGES 20:13

When we dig in our heels and refuse to do our part to uphold justice, the result will be chaotic. There are consequences to our fuel to fight rather than to seek peace. If we have wronged someone else or if we have played a role in the harming of someone, avoiding responsibility and refusing to seek restorative justice and forgiveness will be to our own downfall.

At any point, we can choose to lay down our pride and humbly seek a peaceful and accountable solution. May we have hearts that are quick to admit our wrongs and promote peace within our communities and homes. Justice is ultimately the Lord's, and he will have his way. But let's be arbiters of his justice in this world, looking for ways to reflect his mercy in every area of life. Then we will know that we are shining as living lights for the Lord.

God of justice, may I never stand in the way of your righteousness in the earth. Keep my heart humble and moldable in your love that others may see it working out in my life and give you praise.

NO MORE CIVIL WAR

Instead, the Benjamites gathered warriors from all their towns
to come to Gibeah and fight their brothers, the Israelites.

JUDGES 20:14

In their stubbornness, the Benjamites' refusal to uphold justice
meant that the other tribes joined in unity to fight against them.
When we are obstinate in pride, refusing to bend our opinions in
the light of truth, we will consequentially be humbled by others.
We cannot stand on our own merit, letting unreasonableness keep
us from the accountability of others, without a fierce fight. Yet, it is
this fight that may just lead to our downfall.

The Lord calls us to unity, not to division. He calls us to rise up in
love, not push others away in offense or defensiveness. He calls
us to live from his higher perspective, according to his law of love
that Jesus showed us. If we want to walk the path of love, we must
remember the key element of humility. Let's be unoffendable, be
open-hearted, and seek justice in all things. We are called to look
for ways to promote peace, not to defend our own kingdoms.

*Unifying Lord, when I am tempted to write another off in
irritation, may I stay grounded and humble in your love that offers
more chances than it takes. Thank you!*

SEEK COUNSEL

Before the battle, the armies of Israel went to the house of God
to seek counsel from God. The Israelites inquired,
"Which tribe gets to go first to battle the Benjamites?"

JUDGES 20:18

In life, we will face many spiritual battles. Some seasons may
feel like an endless barrage of hardship and disappointment.
In these times, as in all times, let us go to the Lord who always
gives perspective for our confusion and clarity for our questions.
Seeking counsel from the wise ones in our lives will serve us well.
Seeking counsel from the Spirit of wisdom is an open door that we
should always walk through.

What problems are you facing today? What are the challenges
that you feel ill-equipped to address? Go to the Lord and reach
out to trusted counsel in your life. You will know the right thing to
do as you let the truth settle into your heart and the Spirit speaks
confidence to your soul. He does not often give a blueprint, but
he does illuminate the next step. Don't wait for the full play-by-
play before you take the next step right in front of you. God will
faithfully guide you as you look to him.

*Wise One, speak to me with your truth and enlighten my mind
with your revelation-light.*

ENCOURAGEMENT TO PERSEVERE

The men of Israel encouraged one another and resumed their battle positions where they had lined up the first day.

JUDGES 20:22

When we are showing up to the challenges in our lives day after day, we may become weighed down by the mounting pressures. When we are discouraged at the lack of movement and breakthrough that we want to see, we can recalibrate in the life-giving presence of our God. Let us share our struggles with those who understand. In community, we will find the encouragement we need to persevere as we take turns speaking life and God's perspective over one another.

When we are filled with encouragement, we are strengthened in our spirit. With this spirit-strength, we can go back to the starting line and face another day and another challenge. With the fresh courage of hope, we partner with God again in the fight of our lives. Let's not forget the importance of relief and encouragement we find in the fellowship of the saints.

Spirit, you are my greatest encouragement. But, oh, how grateful I am for true and loving community in my friends, family, and neighbors. What a gift they are to me!

LET WEEPING LEAD YOU TO THE LORD

After losing again, the entire Israelite army went up
to the house of God, and they sat there fasting
and weeping before Yahweh all day until evening.

JUDGES 20:26

*D*isappointment leads us into grief. When we experience a
crushing defeat, there is nothing to do but mourn. May we not
rush ahead, trying to push through, but may we also not give
up and abandon our hope. In these times of heartbreak and
confusion, let's spend the necessary time grieving with close
friends and with the Lord. The Israelites went together to the house
of God and wept openly before him.

If you have ever grieved a great loss, you know the disorientation
of it. You do not weep for a moment and then move on. It rocks
your whole world. It reduces your capacity to function as you used
to. It may cause you to go into a time of withdrawal. In these times,
may we embrace the grieving and do it openly before the Lord.
He is always present with us, never abandoning us. He is present
in our sadness, and he holds us in our heartbreak.

*Lord, thank you for meeting me in my mourning. I will not pretend
to be okay when I am not, and you don't require it. Surround me
with comfort.*

DON'T GIVE UP

"Should we quit?" Yahweh answered, "Attack!
For tomorrow I will give you the victory!"

JUDGES 20:28

Before you decide to quit, ask the Lord what you should do. He may just say that the time is here and that your victory is imminent. Don't give up because it is hard. Don't abandon your hope because you have been disappointed. This is where it is important to stay close to the Lord and to continue to go to him for help, wisdom, and discernment.

Failure is a part of life, not a character flaw. Even when our choices lead us to failure, there is still so much mercy to greet us. The Lord is the restorer of all things, and he faithfully redeems that which has been torn apart and rendered useless by the world. When he says to not give up, let's hold on to our hope. When he speaks to our hearts to take courage in his promises, let's grab hold of them again and declare them over our circumstances. Don't quit because you're weary. Look to the Lord and listen for his instruction.

God of truth, lead me in your wisdom and speak clearly to my weary heart. Help me to have endurance and tenacity in the troubles of life. You are worthy of my trust.

MOURNING FOR OTHERS

The people came to Bethel and sat until evening before God,
and they raised their voice with groaning and great weeping.

JUDGES 21:2

The kind of weeping and groaning that the Israelites experienced in this verse was the deep grief of their brothers' defeat. Their victory over the Benjamites was not a true triumph. It was also a reason to deeply grieve the disconnection of their tribal identity. They wept on behalf of those whom they loved, even though they had been fighting for justice.

Empathy does not require us to agree with another's opinions. It moves us to consider the experience of the other. In this case, Israel was moved with empathy for the loss that the Benjamites experienced. God's love feels for us all. His mercy moves toward every living person. His compassion is moved deeply for all who suffer, no matter their tribe, their sins, or their affiliations. May we mourn with those who mourn, even when we disagree with what they have done. In doing so, we reflect the great mercy-heart of God our Father.

Merciful Father, may my heart never grow cold against another human being. May I see them with your eyes, making space to feel what they must be feeling. Comforter, be their comfort, and may my intercession move heaven on their behalf.

DIVIDED AND DISHEARTENED

They said, "Yahweh, the true God of Israel,
we have lost one of our own tribes today.
Why has this happened to Israel?"

JUDGES 21:3

In the aftermath of tragedy, we may find ourselves broken and at a loss for how to move forward. When we are divided and disheartened, as the Israelites were in this moment, what do we do? May we take all of our heartbreak and our confusion to the Lord. He can handle it all.

The true God of Israel is the true God of the nations. He is not only moved in love toward one people group. He is moved toward us all, for we are all his handiwork and creation. We can come as boldly before him with our hearts wide open as any other, for Jesus has paved the way for one and all to the Father's throne room. Let's follow him into his presence. Let's open the doors of our hearts and let his healing oil flow in. He will unify, restore, and encourage us. He is our hope and our redemption.

Jesus, I come to the Father through you today. I hold nothing back. Meet me with the overwhelmingly healing mercy of your heart and love me to life once again.

MOVED WITH EMPATHY

Even so, the Israelites had compassion for their brothers of the tribe of Benjamin and were grieved deeply over their loss.

JUDGES 21:6

*E*ven when we build boundaries that we know are good for us, it does not mean that we close off our hearts to the plight of others. We can grieve with them and still know that we did what needed to be done. May we allow the passion of God's heart to enlarge our own, even when it causes discomfort within us.

When we are overcome with the compassion of the Father for others, we are moving in empathy. We are compelled by his kindness. As we allow God's love to move us, even in heartbreak for another's loss, we grow in the expansion of his kingdom of love. Apathy is stagnant. Hatred puts up walls between us. Love is a force that continually moves us toward one another in understanding. We are never without God's overwhelming compassion toward us. As we clothe ourselves in the abundance of his mercy-heart, our relationships will also be covered and transformed.

Merciful One, thank you for your love that accounts for us all. Move my heart with what moves yours today.

CHANGE OF HEART

> "How can we provide wives for the few survivors since we have sworn by Yahweh that we will not give any of our daughters as wives for them?"
>
> JUDGES 21:7

God's mercy is large enough to account for the mistakes we make. In their fury, Israel vowed to never let the survivors of Benjamin intermarry with their own. In the light of compassion in the following days, they regretted that vow. They wanted to figure out a way to offer restoration to their fallen tribe.

God knows our propensity to rush into making covenants, and Jesus talked about this in his Sermon on the Hillside in Matthew 5. He addressed our uncertainty and regret when he instructed that we not swear by anything, either on heaven or on earth. We should just let our yes be yes and our no be no. Then, if we change our mind when we have cooler tempers and clearer minds, we will not be bound by what we vowed in haste. May we take the advice of Jesus seriously and apply it to our lives. He always has room for redemption and creative solutions, but he also gives us wisdom to avoid foolish situations.

Wise Jesus, thank you for always providing a way for redemption. May I move in your wisdom and not make rushed decisions that I will regret.

GODLY SORROW

The people were remorseful and had compassion on the tribe of
Benjamin because Yahweh had taken out a tribe of Israel.

JUDGES 21:15

*G*odly sorrow leads us to repentance. "God designed us to
feel remorse over sin," as 2 Corinthians 7:10 states. That remorse
produces repentance that leads to our deliverance. It leads us
to victory. When we are standing in the victory of a humbly
submitted heart to God, there is no room for regret.

With remorse comes compassion. They go hand in hand. We
have compassion toward others because we understand that we
all fall short of the perfect glory of the Lord. No one is sinless. No
one is without flaw or fault. In Jesus, we are all made new in the
restorative power of his love. He is the one who qualifies, purifies,
and makes us right with God. His power is at work in the same
measure in each of our lives. After godly sorrow leads us back to
renewed relationship with our wonderful Savior, his resurrection
power renews, refreshes, and liberates us.

*Jesus, lead me to your heart with love. Draw me in with kindness.
I cannot make it through on my own. I need you. I turn from the
pull of sin and shame, and I come to you.*

FOUNDATIONAL TERRITORY

The Israelites dispersed by tribes and families,
and they went out from there to their own territories.

JUDGES 21:24

After peace had returned to Israel, each of the tribes went off to their own land. They took their families and went home. In the peacetimes of our lives, we get to go to our own territories—the places where God has sent us to raise up our families in love. We get to sow into our own fields where we will one day reap a harvest. We get to dig into the blessing of peace and build up our lives on the foundation of his favor.

May we never take for granted the beauty of peace in our lives. May we not dream about the times of struggle that have passed and the heightened emotional states we were in at the time. May we learn to treasure the slow pace of peacetime. We can learn to live in each moment, soaking in the warmth of laughter, hard work, and rest with our families, friends, and communities. May we not hang around in someone else's territory, longing for what they have, when we have been given our own.

Father, I want to work the land I've been given and love the life I have. Teach me to value peace and to promote harmony.

EACH TO THEIR OWN WAY

In those days, Israel had no king,
and everyone did whatever they wanted to do.

JUDGES 21:25

Without the unifying force of a strong leader, each will go to their own way, doing what they want to do. This was true in the days of the Israelites after the time of the judges, and this still rings true of humanity today.

Thankfully, we have a King in Jesus Christ. He is the Son of the Father of all things, Emmanuel, our Redeemer. Under his leadership, we are unified in his love and liberated by his mercy-kindness. We are instructed with his wisdom and given direction in his fellowship. Instead of each going to our own way, let's yield our lives to the King of kings. The worthy One can be trusted with our hearts and lives. Let's crown him in our lives and let him rule as King of our hearts.

King of kings, I yield my life to you, and my heart is yours in surrender. I trust your leadership more than any other. I know that you are the way, the truth, and the life, and I give my life's leadership to you. Guide me with your gracious wisdom.

IN TIMES OF UNCERTAINTY

During the era when champion-deliverers ruled in Israel,
a severe famine overtook the land.

RUTH 1:1

When times of uncertainty hit our lives and turn everything on its head, we may find that we move in directions that we had not thought of before. A famine is no small thing. It is not a couple days of dry weather. A famine ravages a land for extended periods of time, sometimes years, not only drying up the resources that were there but also threatening the livelihoods and very lives of those in its grip.

Have you ever found yourself in a time where you could not foresee how you would provide for your family? Did every dream or picture you had of your future seem to be wiped out with the unavoidable trouble of a large-scale disturbance? When these times come, God is as faithful and secure as he ever was or will be. May we find strength, peace, and joy in the fellowship of his Spirit that goes with us into any and every circumstance. May our hope remain anchored in the overwhelming goodness of our God.

Good Father, I trust you even in the uncertainty of a cloudy future. When troubles come, I will press closer to your presence, relying on you for help. I trust you.

IMMIGRANTS

Elimelech, a man of importance, left Bethlehem and immigrated
to the country of Moab. He took with him his wife Naomi
and their two sons, Mahlon and Chilion.

RUTH 1:2

What does the word *immigrant* conjure up in your mind? What
is your gut reaction to hearing the term? Take this opportunity to
let the Lord, in his love, shine his light on your heart. He is faithfully
working to unveil the hidden biases we have and purify our hearts
in his mercy. The story of Ruth begins with the immigration of a
Hebrew man and his family to a different country. There, in that
nation, we do not know how they were received or whether their
experience was a good one.

Elimelech moved his family to Moab in the midst of a famine. He
was a man of importance in Bethlehem, so we can assume that
it was a sacrifice for them to leave. Through the lens of hindsight,
we can see how God used his decision to affect history through
Naomi and Ruth. May we allow the compassion of Jesus to fill us
with openness to our friends and neighbors who have emigrated
from far-off lands.

*Jesus, I open my heart to those who are different from me,
grateful that you know us all through and through.*

LEFT ALONE

Elimelech died and left his widow Naomi
alone with her two sons.

RUTH 1:3

*I*n the wake of her husband's death, Naomi was left alone with
her two sons. She, a widow and a foreigner, raised them there in
Moab. Can you imagine what that was like for her? She did not
have her community of friends from home, they probably spoke a
different language, and she had just lost her husband. How alone
she must have felt!

When we go through trying times of great distress and we feel
alone and ill-equipped to handle it, we can know the great grace-
strength of the Spirit that never abandons us. Even when we find
ourselves in strange lands with different customs, even when we are
grieving a great loss without trusted comforters to depend on, even
when all is foreign and incredibly isolating, we are never alone.
God understands our deep grief, and he is our close Comforter. He
is a steady support and a great relief for our weary souls.

*Comforter, thank you for being with me in my grief and for
comforting me in my loneliness. Make yourself even more real
to me.*

CONNECTION TO OTHERS

The two sons both married Moabite women, Orpah and Ruth.

RUTH 1:4

*E*ven though Israelite men were not supposed to intermarry with other nations, Naomi's sons both married Moabites. The family became connected to the local community and culture through this marriage in ways that they hadn't been before.

God is so very gracious toward us. His abounding love and kindness welcome those who were excluded by sin. His mercy invites those into his family who were once outside of his kingdom. There is a place for everyone who turns to him for help. No one is disqualified from his mercy. May we look to connect with others in ways that honor God and extend mercy instead of shutting people out with fear. God is bigger than our understanding, and his lavish love outshines every apprehension we may have. As we honor the Lord with our lives, love will be the force that connects us. He meets us even in our compromise and threads his mercy-kindness through our lives when we submit to him.

Lord, above all, may your love be what connects me to others. I trust you to use even my mistakes to pave a way for your mercy. Thank you!

EVEN MORE ALONE

Mahlon and Chilion also died and left Naomi
all alone without husband or sons.

RUTH 1:5

*N*aomi had already lost her husband, but when her sons both died, she felt completely alone and adrift. What a hard loss! Her entire family was gone. What a deep grief she must have felt. When life beats us down and it looks as though more is taken away than is given, we cannot do anything but mourn. Those who have experienced profound loss know the impact of this grief. Naomi knew, Job knew it, and many of us do too.

Looking through the lens of history, we can see the end where Naomi could not. In our deep grief, it feels like we are in a cavern of darkness. Where does the light come in? Surely, it does over time. But there is no escaping the visceral experience of loss. We simply must walk through it. We know that there is redemption in Naomi's story. We know what's coming. Let's take hope in our dark nights of grief that there is redemption for us as well.

Redeemer, I need your presence in my loneliness and pain. I depend on you to get me through. Be near, Lord, and breathe hope into my heart.

GLIMMER OF HOPE

Sometime later, Naomi heard that Yahweh had visited his people and blessed them with an abundant harvest; so she decided to leave Moab with her daughters-in-law.

RUTH 1:6

*T*he goodness of God to send rain to his people, even as they did whatever they wanted to do in these days, is a reflection of his unrelenting mercy. His character never changes. In hearing about the harvest her people were experiencing, perhaps Naomi felt a glimmer of hope rise within her chest. Just enough to redirect her home. Whatever motivation it was that moved her, she felt the pull to return home.

When we hear about the Lord moving in a region, city, or church, do we not feel a small glimmer of hope within us as well? That God is not done with us yet? The sun still rises every day. The rains of spring still refresh the earth. The cycles of the earth do not cease. And so, the cycles of our lives continue to turn. May we follow the hope, knowing that there is more for us still, even in our barrenness.

Faithful One, your loyal love draws me to you time and time again. I return to you today, with hope alive in my heart. Meet me with the goodness of your presence.

JOURNEY OF RETURNING

With Orpah and Ruth at her side,
Naomi began her journey to return to the land of Judah.

RUTH 1:7

*N*aomi began the journey of returning home with her daughters-in-law in tow. As a band of three, they gathered their belongings and started the excursion that would lead them back to the land of Naomi's relatives. Perhaps you find yourself in a situation where you are transitioning from a place of barrenness to the promise of abundance. The draw to stay where you are is no longer enough because the pull to leave is stronger.

Whether you find yourself on a spiritual journey or a physical one, may you take only what is necessary. Leave behind that which does not suit you any longer. Don't hold to things that will only weigh you down. Count the cost of the journey, knowing you will have to carry these things with you on the way. Take only what is meaningful, what serves you, and what you feel led to. God will provide the rest. Trust him to do it. He goes with you on the path of your journey, and you have his leadership and help.

Constant One, thank you for your presence and wisdom that leads me in love and teaches me in truth. As I journey with you, be near and speak hope to my heart.

BLESSING OF RELEASE

Soon Naomi said to them, "Each of you, go back to your mother's home. May Yahweh show his loyal love and kindness to you—the same kindness you've shown to me and to those who have died."

RUTH 1:8

*A*long the way, Naomi realized that her journey home was hers to take. She did not want to dictate to her daughters-in-law what they should do. She was grateful for their companionship and kindness toward her and her sons. She clearly loved them deeply. But she also understood that if they went with her, they would have minimal opportunities.

Naomi recognized that bringing them to her homeland would make them foreigners. She had lived that life; she knew what that was like. Perhaps she wanted to spare them that experience of hardship. Instead, she released them with a blessing to return to their mother's homes and to go back to their families. There, they could at least be with their own people and the ones who raised them. When we love people deeply, we offer them the opportunity to choose what they will, wanting what is best for them.

Lord, I want to love like you—giving freedom of choice and loving without expecting anything in return. May I release those I love into their own way, just as Naomi did.

REDEMPTIVE BLESSING

"May Yahweh give you another husband
and cause you to find rest in a happy home."

RUTH 1:9

In her release of her daughters-in-law, Naomi also spoke a blessing of restoration and redemption over them. She blessed them, not only to return to their homes, but to also have a chance for happiness. She wanted them to have families. Perhaps she felt the loneliness of her own widowhood and wanted better for them.

May we learn to bless others when we release them. Not everyone in our lives will be with us through the long haul, and that's okay. May we bless them as they go, praying that God would go with them and lead them into abundance in their own lives. May we release prayers of redemption over those who have experienced loss instead of pitying them. May we be those who lift others up, even in our parting of paths.

Redeemer, you are the God who takes our sorrows and sows seeds of joy with our tears. Teach me to bless those who are in mourning, knowing that my direction may be different from theirs.

HEART-WRENCHING GOODBYE

Naomi tenderly embraced Orpah and Ruth
and kissed them goodbye, but they wailed and sobbed.

RUTH 1:9

*H*ave you ever had a goodbye with someone whom you knew you probably wouldn't see again? This is the type of goodbye that Naomi, Ruth, and Orpah were having. In the parting of their ways, they knew that this was probably the last time they would be together. And, even if they would reunite, it would not be under the same circumstances. They had lived together and mourned together. They had become family.

Let us be people who honor our relationships, even in goodbyes. May we not be quick to rush past the tears and the tender embraces. May we honor each other in our sadness, being true to the breadth of the moment and the loss that comes with a significant farewell. This, too, was another level of grief for these women. Even though new beginnings hold with them the promise of hope, there is also a level of heartache in a goodbye.

Loving Lord, thank you for the tenderness of your presence. Help me to honor my relationships and seasons of my life when I move into new places. May I not hold back from the sorrow, while still being able to recognize the hope ahead.

LONGING FOR MORE

Through their tears, they said to her,
"No! We want to be with you
and go with you to your people."

RUTH 1:10

In their deep mourning, Ruth and Orpah did not want to leave Naomi. Perhaps they did not want to imagine a different life with others who couldn't quite understand what they had been through together. When there is an invitation to a different path, we may hesitate to embrace the idea of change and opportunity.

In goodbyes, and even in grief, there is a longing for more than we've had the opportunity to experience. There are what-ifs and if-onlys. This longing is not ill-placed or wrong. It is deeply seated within each one of us. From this place, we must weigh what that longing reflects in us. Do we honor the longings while recognizing that it is best for us to move into something else, or are those longings meant to be honored in a different way? May we press into the presence of the Lord for his wisdom when we face a fork in the road of life and feel pulled in different directions. He will give us clarity of heart and mind.

Wise One, when there is longing in my heart for more, give me discernment with what to do with it. I trust your help.

MAKES NO SENSE

"My daughters, you must go back," Naomi answered.
"Why do you want to come with me?
Do you think I could have sons again to give you new husbands?"

RUTH 1:11

*N*aomi could offer no inheritance to her daughters-in-law. She had nothing from her husband's family to give them. It made no logical sense for either of them to return to her homeland with her. Their best chance at a new life and a new family was to return to their own homes.

Logic will sometimes help us make decisions. Other times, logic can hinder us in following our hearts as they pull us on the path of the Lord. Either way, the choices that are in front of us are always ours to make. May we use not only common sense but also the Spirit of the Lord as our help and discernment. The ways of the Lord sometimes look foolish to others, and they do not always make sense to the logical mind. And that's okay. Let us look to the Lord for help when we need clarity and direction. He is a faithful guide and friend. And above all, he is the God who uses our choices and weaves his mercy-thread through them to bring restoration and redemption.

Lord, I trust your wisdom more than the logic of this world.

A HOPELESS CASE

"Turn around my daughters and go back home,
for I'm too old to marry again."

RUTH 1:12

Surely, we know that in Jesus, nothing is hopeless. In her grief, Naomi could see no hope for her daughters-in-law to come with her. She had no great expectations that the Lord would sow blessings in her life again. She felt hopeless, though we can see through hindsight that there was hope around the bend.

When we feel as if our situations are hopeless, may we remember the saints that have gone before us that have felt the same way. God's faithfulness always shines through. His promises are never abandoned, and even when we cannot sense him working, God is working all things together for the good of those who love him and are submitted to his kingdom ways (Romans 8:28). There is nothing we could ever experience that cannot be restored or redeemed, and the Lord will shine a light of hope to those still in the dark. May we look beyond our circumstances to the strong anchor of hope that never moves.

Faithful One, I know that in you nothing and no one is hopeless. I trust your redemptive love to turn my mourning to dancing and my sorrow to joy. I know you will make something beautiful out of the mess I'm in.

Too Bitter

"No, my daughters, you must not return with me.
My life is too bitter for you to share it with me
because Yahweh has brought calamity to my life!"

RUTH 1:13

The harshness of Naomi's feelings in her deep grief help to normalize what we experience in mourning. There are tragedies that wipe out our hope, and yet God is still faithful. Though we cannot perceive his goodness in the aftermath of trauma, God is still good, merciful, and true.

Who of us, when we are in the trenches of grieving heavy losses in life, have not felt like a discouragement to those around us? Naomi's statement of "my life is too bitter for you to share it with me" reflects the deep sorrow of tragic loss. Did this make Naomi faithless? No. Did it mean that God could no longer work in her life? Also, no. May we take encouragement from the story of Naomi's struggle, knowing that God sees, understands, and still works through us, even when our lives seem too bitter to share with anyone.

Sovereign Lord, there truly is no one else like you. You move on the behalf of the heartbroken and the vulnerable. You provide for widows and sow redemption into each of our stories. Thank you.

WHICH WAY WILL YOU GO?

When they heard Naomi's words, Orpah and Ruth wailed and sobbed again. Then Orpah embraced and kissed her mother-in-law goodbye and went back home.

RUTH 1:14

There was no denying the choice before them when Naomi kept encouraging Ruth and Orpah to return to their families. She had laid out her case, detailing the hopelessness of returning to Judah with her. There was nothing for them there.

Orpah heeded Naomi's advice and encouragement and embraced her mother-in-law for the last time and then returned home to her family. This was her choice, and there was nothing wrong with it. We know that Ruth's choice was different, and the Lord use her loyalty to Naomi to bless them both. We do not know what happened to Orpah, but we can assume that God was faithful to her as well, if she lived a life of submission to him. His mercy is consistent and carried out in faithfulness to his word. May we weigh our decisions in the light of the Lord and his wisdom, but in the end, we can trust him to be with us, no matter what.

God of love, thank you for your freedom that allows me to make choices knowing that your mercy is big enough to meet me in the consequences of them. Go with me, Lord.

CLING TIGHTLY

Ruth clung tightly to Naomi
and refused to let go of her.

RUTH 1:14

*R*uth was bonded to Naomi in such a deep and devoted way that she could not imagine leaving her. She clung tightly to Naomi, refusing to let go of her and to turn away from her. It is a picture of how we can cling devotedly to the Lord. In a sense, Ruth's clinging to Naomi was her entering into a covenant with her mother-in-law.

When we cling tightly to the Lord, devoting our lives to him, we embrace him and refuse to turn back to our old lives. When we choose to stay and follow the Lord rather than going back to the familiarity of old patterns, we are creating a covenant of devotion to the Lord. He then leads us to his home, his kingdom, and we become his. May we cling tightly to our Lord God.

Lord, my heart clings to you, and I devote my life to you. Lead me to your land, in your ways, and to your kingdom. I choose you above everything else I've known. It is you.

LIVE BY CONVICTION

Naomi said, "Ruth, listen. Your sister-in-law is going back to Moab
to her people and to her gods. Now go with her."

RUTH 1:15

*N*aomi resisted Ruth's devotion to her, and she encouraged
her to go back to her own family, her own people, and her former
way of life. She encouraged her to return to her roots. And yet, we
know that the pull of the familiar was not what Ruth wanted. She
didn't want to return to her family's home. She counted Naomi as
dearer to her than her own flesh and blood.

May we live by the conviction of our hearts and souls, even in
the face of those who are trying to reason with our minds. May
we stay strong in our principles and live according to them. The
wisdom of God is wiser than the insight of the world. May we trust
his faithfulness even in the face of the unknown. Ruth counted
the unknowns ahead of her as worth the price to pay to remain in
close companionship with Naomi. May we count the cost of our
conviction and yet press ahead in it anyway.

Faithful One, I know that you are undeterred in your devotion.
May I also remain resolute in mine.

NOBLE CHOICE

Tearfully, Ruth insisted, "Please don't ask me again to leave you!
I want to go with you and stay with you."

RUTH 1:16

*R*uth's response to Naomi's encouragement to leave her was full of sorrow and tension. She wanted to go with Naomi, and here she was, trying to convince her mother-in-law of her devotion. Through tears, she begged Naomi to stop resisting and let her accompany her. Ruth needed Naomi as much as Naomi needed the companionship of her daughter-in-law. In full knowledge of her choice, Ruth insisted that she would not leave Naomi.

When someone has made a resolute choice, where no one can convince them of a better option, what use is there in arguing? Each of us is responsible for our own decisions, and we cannot control the will of another. Let us give grace to those who are making choices we do not understand, and let's stay strong in our own convictions while communicating the passion with which we are walking in them. Let us be devoted to our values, and let's honor the values that others are walking in as well.

Holy One, I am grateful that I never need explain myself or motives to you. Give me grace to communicate well with those around me.

I Will Go Too

"Wherever you go, I will go;
wherever you live, I will live.
Your people will now be my people,
and your God will be my God."

RUTH 1:16

When we leave our old lives behind and follow Christ on the path of his life, love, and peace, we are made new. Our vision is forward—eyes fixed on Christ and his coming kingdom. Our eyes resolutely look ahead to the promises of God. Wherever he goes, we go. Where he lives, we live. His people become our people, and he becomes our God, our head, our leader, and our Redeemer.

When we find faithful friends in this life, they are gifts from God. Those who encourage us, who love us wherever we are, and who are committed to our development, and we to theirs, are special treasures. Let us develop deep relationships with loyal friends who encourage us in love and life. There is strength in communion with others who are devoted to the Lord and who live lives that we want to emulate. May we devote our lives to God and to one another in the same kind of love that Ruth showed Naomi.

Almighty God, thank you for the gift of friendship. Thank you for your devotion toward us. I submit to your ways.

UNDYING DEVOTION

"Wherever you die, I will die there, too;
that's where your people will bury me—next to you."

RUTH 1:17

The kind of devotion Ruth displayed was not only to follow Naomi in life but also in death. The old Ruth died that day she devoted herself to Naomi. In the same way, we, too, have been crucified with Christ. His cross was our cross, and his death was ours. We have also been raised to life in the resurrection power of Jesus. His new life is our renewal.

When we lay our lives down at the cross of Christ, we come away completely made new. His resurrection life is ours. We follow him to the ends of the earth, if we must. Yet, here he is, with us even now through his Spirit. The undying devotion of Jesus is our ultimate example of laid-down-love. And we see this foreshadowed through Ruth in the Scriptures. Let us follow him, for surely beyond death there is life everlasting.

Jesus, thank you for your sacrifice and for your undying love. I gladly give you my life, and I lay it down so that I may be raised up in you.

SOLEMN VOW

"Nothing but death itself will separate me from you,
so help me God!"

RUTH 1:17

Ruth's solemn vow to Naomi was a covenant of love until death. She promised to never leave her, to follow her and stay with her until one or both of them was gone. There is no stronger vow that one can make. We often consider this kind of vow made through marriage—till death do us part. This is what Ruth was vowing to Naomi: to be her companion for life. What a beautiful picture of love.

May we know the significance of the vows we make and know that loving devotion can be displayed through other relationships besides marriage. There is beauty in a romantic partnership, but there are also equal amounts of beauty in the loyalty of a friend or a family member. There is a deep expression of love we can experience in any close relationship. May we value these in our own lives and honor them in others.

God, thank you that your love is larger than romantic love. May I experience the depths of your love through every close relationship I have in life.

HEART SET

When Naomi realized that Ruth's heart was set on going with her,
she said nothing more.

RUTH 1:18

When we set our hearts on something, we cannot be talked out of it. When our minds are made up, it is almost impossible to change it. This may not be true of everything in life, but surely it is when we are making a decision based on our core values. There are moments in life that will forever mark us and change our trajectories because of the decisions we make. Let us keep our hearts devoted to the Lord in all things. When we do, everything else will align in his mercy.

Instead of trying to talk someone out of something they have their heart set on, let's let them follow through in their own way. There is no use arguing with someone who has no intention of changing their mind. Just as we set our hearts on what seems right to us, others can and will do the same. Let's learn to support each other and know when to simply be silent on the matter.

Lord, my heart is set on you, above all else. Lead me in your love and work out the details that I cannot in your wisdom.

HOMECOMING

Naomi and Ruth traveled together from Moab until they came to Bethlehem. The entire town was buzzing when they heard they had arrived!

RUTH 1:19

When news spread of Naomi's return to Bethlehem, the whole town was astounded by the news. They were beside themselves over it. It had been a while since they had seen her last, perhaps about ten years. Have you ever returned home or to a familiar place in your childhood after a long time away? It is strange how it feels both utterly familiar and different at the same time.

The reception we receive from those we shared life with so long ago may be like a warm hug after a cold night. How wonderful to be reunited with long lost friends. The questions that follow may cause us to bristle in some ways. The return of Naomi was not filled with joy on her part. She returned without her husband and sons. She had nothing left except for Ruth. Her homecoming, though it was probably sweet in some ways, was also bitter. We will only ever find our true home in Christ.

Lord, I'm grateful for my home in you. I never have to explain myself to you or catch up. Thank you for earthly reunions, even when they are a mix of joyful and sorrowful.

GRIEF'S MARK

"Please don't call me Naomi anymore," she insisted. "Instead, call me Marah, because Almighty God has dealt me a bitter blow."

RUTH 1:20

Naomi could not hide her hopeless sorrow from the women who greeted her. She did not want to be reminded of the meaning of her name, which was "pleasant." She did not feel as though her life was pleasant. She instead asked them to call her Marah, meaning "bitter." She had sipped from the bitter waters of grief, and she could not sense the sweetness that was yet to come.

The anguish of our souls in mourning leaves a lasting mark on our hearts. We are forever changed by the loss of those we love, though there is certainly redemption in Christ. Naomi could not yet know that there would be restoration to her line. She could not hope for something so sweet to come out of something so bitter. God's grace meets us where we are, even in the harshness of our sorrow and agony. He still works out what we cannot dare to hope for in his love. He is just that good.

Restorer, I'm so grateful that your faithfulness is not dependent on my faith. Let your mercy wash over even the areas I cannot imagine being redeemed in my life. I believe that you are good.

IDENTITY CRISIS

"When I left here, my heart was full and content with my family, but Yahweh has brought me back empty and destitute. Why call me by my name, 'Pleasant,' when Yahweh has opposed me, and Almighty God has brought me so much trouble?"

RUTH 1:21

In the tragedy of her circumstances, Naomi went through an identity crisis. Everything she had known was turned on its head. Perhaps everything she believed and hoped about God had been too. She struggled to understand where she stood with God. In fact, she believed that God had opposed her and, in so doing, that she was cursed.

We know that her understanding was not God's actual attitude toward her. He faithfully restored her family line and offered a hope that she could not imagine on her own. Yet, she still could not reconcile the trouble she had found herself in, along with all the pain of her suffering, with her identity in God. In the light of our circumstances, do we also question our identity? May we find ourselves in the faithfulness of God, for his love will never fail. Not even in our misery.

Merciful Father, may the roots of my identity be firmly established in your love. When I don't know why I'm experiencing what I am, may I still know that I am yours.

EARLY HARVESTTIME

Naomi returned to her village with Ruth,
her Moabite daughter-in-law. They arrived in Bethlehem
just as the barley harvest had begun.

RUTH 1:22

*T*he season of famine had ended in the land, and the season of harvest had begun. This happened to coincide with the time of the Feast of Passover. Here, in the barley harvest, Naomi and Ruth found themselves surrounded by abundance. Though they still had nothing, the land itself was bursting with grain.

In certain seasons of our lives, whether we have been sowing, planting, or reaping, we get to partake in the early harvest of the lands where we live. The area's abundance becomes our own. When cities are prosperous, the inhabitants of that city reap the benefits. When there is spiritual abundance in the harvest, those who are around during that time also reap the rewards. May we know the seasons and the times we are in, and may we give thanks no matter what season it is. There is always a reason to give thanks.

Provider, you bring the rains, and you make the sun shine on the earth. Wildflowers grow and pastures flourish under your hand. I trust you with my barren seasons and in seasons of plenty. Your love remains the same.

HONORABLE AND PROMINENT

Naomi's deceased husband, Elimelech, had a very wealthy relative, an honorable and prominent man in Bethlehem named Boaz.

RUTH 2:1

*B*oaz was more than noted in the community of Bethlehem. He was wealthy, but he was also a man of honor and integrity. He was highly esteemed within the city, full of substance and known as a victorious and powerful man. We have all known powerful people, but how many of us have known powerful people full of integrity? It seems to be a rare occurrence, indeed.

No matter our level of physical wealth, we can build our soul-wealth by being people of our word, using wisdom in our dealings, and honoring others. As we fellowship with the Spirit, we build an orchard that produces his fruit in our lives. Let's be sure to align our choices with his kingdom ways, extending mercy, kindness and upholding justice with honesty and integrity. We will be known as lovers of God by the way we live, just as Boaz was known.

Mighty God, I honor you with my life and choices today. You are the one I want to imitate in life. May your love guard, keep, and propel me in all my decisions and dealings.

HOW TO HELP

One day Ruth the Moabite said to Naomi,
"Let me go to the fields and pick up the leftover grain."

RUTH 2:2

*W*hen we are in transitions in life and we find ourselves with nothing to do, do we not look for ways to be useful? Ruth knew that she could offer to help her and Naomi's situation by doing something about it. She was not ambitious in her plan, but she saw an opportunity that could help feed them. She used ingenuity, although it was a simple and humble solution to their dilemma.

When we look for ways to help, we will find them. We don't need to wait for the perfect opportunity to do something about it. Desperation leads to creative solutions, and this was true for Ruth's idea. She was compelled to do something to help Naomi. May we take the small steps we see in front of us, humbling ourselves in the process. Either the path will open up as we tread down it, or we will reroute along another one. Either way, direction often comes in movement, not in trying to forecast what could happen along the way.

Spirit, you are my helper in all things. Thank you! I take small steps of faith and trust you to lead and direct me along the way.

A Shot in the Dark

"Maybe someone will be kind enough
to let me gather the grain he leaves behind."

RUTH 2:2

In thinking about going to the fields to pick up leftover grain, Ruth ventured that she might find grace with someone. She and Naomi were both widows, and in their society, this often meant that they would be shown kindness because of their situation. Because they had no husbands or fathers to care for them, others could take that opportunity to offer them help, even in simply letting them pick up leftover grain after the harvesters had already gone through.

Is there an area where you feel as if you are taking a shot in the dark, hoping it will land where it needs to? The Lord is all-seeing, all-knowing, and all-caring. He can direct us confidently even when we cannot see the way. He is gentle in his leadership, and he will help us when we have no other hope. He is a Good Shepherd, gathering us in and providing for our needs. May we take the steps we feel led to by his Spirit and trust him to give us grace with others.

Gracious God, thank you for leading me in love all the days of my life. I trust you.

PORTION OF PROVISION

Ruth went to the fields to gather the grain the reapers left behind.

RUTH 2:3

In the book of Deuteronomy, God had commanded Israel to care for the poor, specifically through leaving the fallen grain behind after the reapers went through the fields once. This grain was to be left for the foreigner, the fatherless, and the widow to collect. The fact that Boaz upheld this command was a testament to the covenant faithfulness he exemplified. It also was reflective of the mercy-kindness of the Lord to provide for the poor and the needy.

This command to leave behind the remnants of the harvest was also a reminder to Israel that they were once slaves in Egypt who depended on the generosity of Yahweh to feed them. As he had provided for them, so, too, could the Israelites provide for each other. We have this same opportunity today—to care for the foreigner, the widow, and the orphan. May we give out of the generosity of our abundance, not hoarding our wealth and resources to ourselves. God gives freely and provides for us, so we should also freely give and provide for the needs of others.

Provider, thank you for your care for the vulnerable. I will not hoard my resources to myself. Help me to reflect your generosity through every area of my life.

JUST SO

It just so happened that she found herself working at the edges of a field belonging to Boaz of the family of Elimelech.

RUTH 2:3

*T*he fact that Ruth ended up working at the edges of a field belonging to Boaz, a relative of Naomi's, was a reflection of God's kindness. What we see as chance, God used to bring restoration and redemption to both Ruth and Naomi.

Have you ever experienced something that just seemed to be a lucky coincidence? How did it benefit you in the end? May we attribute the glorious goodness of our chances to the faithfulness of the Lord who keeps all of his promises. He is loyal to his word, and he works all things together for the good of those who love him. Even though Naomi was deep in bitter grief and Ruth was a foreigner, he was faithful to provide and care for them in marvelously merciful ways. As he has done, so will he continue to do today.

Faithful One, I recognize your fingerprints of kindness through the chances that work in my favor in life. I give you praise for your kindness toward me. I will live with gratitude on my lips and overflowing from my heart. Thank you!

November

Surveyor of the Harvest

At that moment, Boaz came from Bethlehem to survey his harvest.
He greeted the harvesters, "May Yahweh be with you."

RUTH 2:4

*J*ust as Boaz went out to his fields to survey his harvest, Jesus also came from Bethlehem to bless his harvesters. Those who take his gospel to the nations are present-day harvesters, and the Lord watches over them. His blessing goes with them, and he surveys the harvest fields of the world—the fields that are ripe and ready.

There is a global harvest of souls ready to receive the Lord and his loving redemption. May we live with his gospel truth on our lips and reflected in our lives. Let's invite his Holy Spirit power to move through us as we pray and work for his kingdom to come to earth as it is in heaven. The fields are ripe. Are we willing to go out and do the work of harvesting?

Jesus, you watch over the fields of the nations. As you do, I heed your instructions to sow, to tend, and to collect, depending on the season. My life is yours, Lord. I am at your service.

NOTICED

Noticing Ruth, Boaz asked his foreman in charge of the harvesters,
"Who is that young woman over there?"

RUTH 2:5

No matter where we are in this life or how difficult our circumstances are, Jesus sees us. He takes notice of us, and the Holy Spirit keeps us company. There is nowhere we could hide from his presence, and there is not a single place we could run that we would escape his watchful care.

When we feel as if we are all alone, fighting to just make it through another day, may we know the present power and comfort of the company of the Spirit. Jesus does not lose track of us, and the Spirit is like the foreman under Boaz who equips and places each believer in the harvest fields where we will be the most effective. He puts us where we need to be, and he gives us all we need to do the work at hand. What a good and faithful help he is!

Jesus, thank you for knowing my life better than I do. Thank you for your Spirit that empowers and equips me for what needs to be done. I rely on you in all things.

NO NEED TO HIDE

The foreman answered, "She's a Moabite girl
who came back with Naomi from the country of Moab."

RUTH 2:6

Though Ruth was a foreigner in Israel, this was not held against her. She could not hide her identity, for Naomi was her mother-in-law, and they were well-known in the area. She probably looked different than the others, as well, having different features and an accent.

When we feel as if we stick out like a sore thumb because of our differences, may we take confidence in the fact that we are made in the image of God. There is no face shape that is better than another. We are unique reflections of a creative and vastly beautiful God. May we gain conviction in who God says we are and lay down every need to make ourselves smaller to fit into another's mold or idea of what is acceptable. God loves diversity. If he didn't, he would not have created such varied expressions of beauty in the world and in humanity. Let's embrace who we are and what makes us unique. There is power in acceptance.

Wondrous One, thank you for how you have created me. Instead of trying to become more like others, I want to be the best expression of myself I can be.

Our Circumstances, God's Faithfulness

"She asked for permission to gather the grain left behind by the reapers. Except for one short break, she's been on her feet working in the field since early this morning."

RUTH 2:7

Ruth did not simply ask to gather the grain behind the reapers at Boaz's field; she then followed through and worked for it. She asked, and then she put in the work. May we learn from this example. When we put hard work in, after being given a green light to go ahead, others will take notice. The foreman had been watching Ruth, and he was impressed with her work ethic enough to tell Boaz about it.

God is faithful to answer us when we cry out to him. Jesus is faithful to give us opportunities when we look for them. As we follow through on our own part, he not only notices, but he also passes on the news to the Father. There is so much opportunity for us in each day to follow through. We don't earn his favor, for he already loves and accepts us. But he does bless the work of our hands as we pour ourselves out for the work that is ours to do.

Faithful Father, thank you for your blessing and your strength. I look to you.

MERCY OVER JUDGMENT

Boaz walked over to Ruth and said, "Listen, my daughter,
don't leave this field to glean somewhere else.
Stay here in my field and follow the young women
who work for me."

RUTH 2:8

*B*oaz graciously offered Ruth an opportunity to follow his
workers throughout the harvest season. He could have just let her
be, but he extended a personal invitation to keep coming back
to benefit from the abundance of his fields. He knew her to be a
hard worker, and though she was a foreigner, he had mercy on
her. He did not judge her circumstances or demand that she go
somewhere else. He was faithful to Yahweh's covenant and even
went a step beyond to show more mercy.

Whenever we come to the Lord, we have his mercy. He does not
judge us or the situations we find ourselves in. He is our merciful
provider, and he extends even more kindness to us than we could
ask for. For all that he does, for all that he provides, for all that he is
in loving-kindness, let us give thanks.

*Merciful King, thank you for your love toward me. You are better
to me than any other, and I will stay close to you.*

PROVISION AND PROTECTION

"Watch my harvesters to see into which fields they go to cut grain, and follow them. When you're thirsty, go and drink from the water jugs that the young men have filled. I've warned the young men not to bother you."

RUTH 2:9

*W*hen we are invited into the family of God, he provides what we need. There is more than enough grain to feed us, there is water to quench our thirst, and there is protection from the meddling of others. We have all that we need in the covering of Jesus Christ. He is both our provision and our protection.

When we are following the Lord, he will give us directions to help us on the way. There will be people he sets in our path who will help us to know which way to go. The community of faithful lovers of God who are already working to bring in the harvest will cue us in where to go when we have no idea otherwise. The Spirit is our Living Water, the source of our refreshment and rejuvenation. There is more than enough in his presence to satisfy us whenever we are weary.

Spirit, you are my abundant portion at all times. Thank you for your presence and your power in my life. I love you!

IN AWE

Astounded, Ruth bowed low with her face to the ground.

RUTH 2:10

*H*ave you ever been so awestruck by another's response that it left you speechless? Have you been overcome by the astonishment of another's generosity? Ruth's response to Boaz's generosity was to bow low to the ground. In worship, we do the same. When we are overcome by the overwhelming mercy-kindness of God, sometimes all we can do is bow low with our faces to the ground.

Jesus is the lifter of our heads. When we humble ourselves in worship, he lifts us up and gives us greater glimpses of his love. There is a never-ending exchange of love in the fellowship of Spirit to spirit and divine heart to earthly heart. We pour out our thanksgiving, and he pours out more love. We thank him for his generosity, and he offers more kindness in his affectionate presence. There is power in the purity of his mercy, and there are incalculable revelations in his heart to uncover. We will find ourselves astounded and in awe time and time again.

Wonderful One, I have never known a love like yours. You are holy and just, and yet you call me your own and wash me in the cleansing flow of your mercy-tide. Thank you!

HUMBLED BY KINDNESS

[She] said to him, "I'm a foreigner.
Why have you been so kind and taken notice of me?"

RUTH 2:10

*R*uth was clearly not expecting the kind of favor that Boaz offered her. She was not only astounded by his gracious response to her, but she was also perplexed by his kindness. She could not understand why he, this wealthy and prominent farmer, would take notice of her, both a foreigner and a widow. She could not keep herself from asking him why he would be so kind.

How much more does God show his consideration of us through the loving-kindness of Jesus? The King of kings takes notice of us, though we are not well-known or well-qualified. He takes the outcasts and the lowly and takes care of them. He takes care of us. He offers us more than leftovers, as we can clearly see through Boaz. He offers us the abundance of his care, kindness, and protection.

Jesus, I am humbled by your kindness toward me. I cannot begin to thank you for all that you have done, are doing, and will do. But thank you, all the same.

SELFLESSNESS

Boaz answered, "I've heard all about what you've done for your mother-in-law since the death of your husband. I know your story."

RUTH 2:11

*B*oaz had already heard the story of Ruth, how she had left her father, mother, and her native land to come to a people and culture that was strange to her. He was impressed by her selflessness. Without her even knowing it, Ruth's reputation preceded her. When we act in the same kind of laid-down-love that Jesus instructed and exemplified, others will take notice.

May we take heart and hope from Ruth's experience. May we be encouraged to continue to lay down our rights and live as radical lovers of God as well as lovers of people. Let's lay aside our regrets and keep moving forward in the mercy of the Lord. He takes notice, and nothing we sacrifice on God's behalf is meaningless. He will use it all for our good and for his glory.

Humble King, I follow your example as servant of all, and I lay down my life in loving submission to you. When I am discouraged, I will keep following you, for you are my hope. I know you are faithful to your people.

No Sacrifice Unseen

"May Yahweh reward you for your sacrifices, and because of what you've done, may you have a full and rich reward from Yahweh, the God of Israel, under whose wings you have come to find shelter!"

RUTH 2:12

We find shelter in the presence of God Almighty. Under his wings, we take refuge. Every sacrifice that we make is observed by the Lord. Not only that, but he also rewards us for each one. When we yield our lives to the Lord, it is like a burnt offering that we present to him. We offer ourselves to him, and he is the fiery passion that consumes us.

May we bless those who sacrificially lay down the familiar in favor of serving another. Ruth sacrificed the comfort of her homeland, her blood relatives, and her customs, and she instead chose to follow her mother-in-law in the love that propelled her. May we know that everything we give up in order to follow the path of Jesus' love will be rewarded in full. He has become our shelter, and he will take care of us, noting every offering of surrender along the way.

Sovereign Lord, I'm grateful that you see, know, and understand the level of the sacrifices I offer to you. I know that in that loss, there will also be glorious gain.

COMFORTING WORDS

Ruth replied, "May I continue to find favor in your sight, kind sir. You have spoken to my heart kind and reassuring words that comfort me, even though I am not as worthy as one of your servant girls."

RUTH 2:13

When the truth is spoken to us in love, affirming both our identity and the sacrifices we have made on the path of life, they are words that both reassure and comfort us. May we also be those who encourage others by calling out the beauty of what we see in them. May we be those who comfort others through the acknowledgment of their sacrifice and of their service. In doing so, we build them up with life-giving words.

In our need, Jesus meets us with his kindness and his provision. His favor is our covering, and his love is the foundation of our worthiness. It is not by our own merit that we find ourselves brought into his abundant kingdom, and yet he honors what we offer him. How wonderful he is. How wonderful it is when we are like him.

Comforter, thank you for your affirming kindness in my life. You are the worthy One, and the One I give my life to. I am indebted to you forever.

UNABASHED FAVOR

At mealtime, Boaz said to her, "Come here and eat with us.
Here is bread, and wine to dip in in."...She ate all she wanted
until she was satisfied—she even had some left over.

RUTH 2:14

*J*ust as Boaz beckoned Ruth to draw near, so Jesus calls us.
His invitation for us is always to come close to him and share in
communion with him. He welcomes us to his banqueting table
and offers us from the fullness of his bounty. His abundance is
our provision. His call is our open invitation. May we share in
the bread and the wine with our Lord Jesus in the practice of
communion.

There, we will find all that we long for and even more left over. We
will eat until we are satisfied, and we will not deplete the provision
of his feast. There is always more. Let's take the Lord at his word
today and come close in holy communion with him. He offers us
the abundance of his love, laid out for us in the bread of his body
and in the wine of his blood. He has sacrificed everything so that
we may know him in fullness.

*Jesus, your favor is astounding. I cannot begin to thank you for
the fellowship of your friendship. I draw near to you once more.*

GRACE TO GLEAN

After she had returned to gather grain, Boaz instructed his young men, "Let her glean even among the standing sheaves, and don't disgrace her."

RUTH 2:15

*B*oaz offered even more grace than he did at first, instructing his young men to let Ruth take barley from the sheaves, as well, and not just from the ground. He offered her even more freedom and, along with it, freedom from shame. Even if she were to take from where she should not have, Boaz made provision for her to do so.

How much more gracious is our Lord Jesus with us? He gives us room in the liberty of his love where we can collect without fear of shame or disgrace. He will not let us be put to shame in his fields, for they belong to him, and we are part of his family. Where we have kept ourselves small out of fear of overstepping, may we grow in confidence knowing that God will cover us with his kindness and vouch for us. There is grace to glean.

Father, thank you for your gracious favor that lets me move in the freedom of your love. I do not fear making a mistake, for I know you will continue to teach me. I look to you and your leadership, and I am under your covering.

EXTRA BLESSINGS

"Pull out from the bundles some handfuls of grain and drop them
on purpose for her to gather, and don't bother her."

RUTH 2:16

*E*ven more than freedom to gather as she would, Boaz then
further instructed his young workers to purposely drop some grain
from their own bundles for Ruth to gather. There was nothing that
said that Boaz needed to do this. He was fulfilling the covenant
law of God's faithfulness to the poor through simply letting Ruth
follow behind his workers and collect the leftover grain.

Yet, how like Jesus and his kingdom this act is. He gives even
more blessings, freely leaving treasures along the path of his love
where we can collect them. He is so much better than we can
comprehend, and yet we discover the lavishness of his love as we
continue to fellowship with him. May we never stop pressing into
his purposes, knowing there is more than enough for us in the vast
expanse of his kingdom. Let's be about our Father's business, for
we will share in his abundance. He is the most magnanimous and
loving leader we could ever imagine.

*Loving Lord, thank you for the extra blessings you set out for me.
I won't leave your fields, and I will keep going after you.*

GENEROUS PORTION

Ruth gathered grain in Boaz's field until evening.
When she threshed out what she had gathered,
it came to more than half a bushel of barley.

RUTH 2:17

After a day's work, Ruth returned with about thirty pounds of barley. That's a lot of grain to collect in one day by hand. It was more than generous. Imagine how long that would last her and Naomi. As we do the work that God has for us to do, the Lord will generously provide for us. Though not every season is a harvest season, we can trust that God will take care of us in every one.

There is always a generous portion of God's presence with us. His storehouses never run dry, and there are no shortages in his love. When we come to him, we find that there is always overflow of love, joy, peace, patience, kindness, and grace. There is more than we could fathom available to us, right here and now, in the communion of Spirit to spirit. The fullness of God is our source and sustenance. His favor is our covering. Let's not give up living for his audience and pleasure, for he is so very good.

God, as I benefit from your generosity, I will sow it into others. Thank you for the abundance of your kingdom.

MORE THAN ENOUGH

> She carried it back to town and showed her mother-in-law how much she had gleaned. Then Ruth also took out the roasted grain she had saved from mealtime and shared it with Naomi.
>
> RUTH 2:18

Imagine the amount of barley that Ruth carried back to Naomi, and then picture what Naomi's reaction must have been. Ruth put in a hard day's work, but the return on her work was far more than she ever could have achieved on her own, without the help of Boaz. When we are about our Father's business, God does the same with what we offer him.

As we partner with his purposes, he blesses the work of our hands with his generous grace and makes the return so much greater than we could have gathered by our own means. There is more than enough to go around for all who are hungry and for all who thirst. There is an abundance of grace for all of us who look to the Lord; it is not a fixed amount. It is always overflowing, always more than enough, always astoundingly abundant.

Generous King, thank you for sharing your abundance with all who look to you for help. Your compassion is amazing.

BOUNTEOUS BLESSINGS

Her mother-in-law asked Ruth, "Where did you gather all this from? In whose field did you work? May Yahweh bless the man who showed you special attention."

RUTH 2:19

*N*aomi knew that whoever's field Ruth had worked in, she had found special favor with them. It was clear in the overabundance of what she brought home that Ruth had been shown special attention. When we bring the bounty of our hard work, coupled with God's blessings, the abundance may surprise others.

When we share the abundance of our return with those close to us, we all get to reap the benefits of the blessing. We all, too, get to share in the wonder of God's provision and celebrate together. When we have received generous portions from the helping hand of others, may we, in turn, bless those who blessed us. There is more than enough joy to go around. Let's take time to celebrate the gifts with those we love, for there is deep joy in the commemoration of an answer to prayer.

Faithful One, thank you for the blessings you pour out on your people. May I not be quick to move on to the next thing but take time to celebrate your faithfulness with friends and family.

HEART OF GOD

Naomi said to Ruth, "Yahweh's loving-kindness
has not left us either through life or through death!"

RUTH 2:20

*N*aomi had been deeply discouraged by the deaths of her husband and sons, to the point where she believed that God had turned against her. She felt the bitterness of lonely grief for a long time, and she felt far from Yahweh, her God. Through the generous provision of Boaz's favor upon Ruth, Naomi's heart opened up in hopeful praise and expectation. What she could not see before now glimmered into life.

When we feel utterly alone in the darkness of despair and we cannot grab hold of the hope we once had, let us take heart from Naomi's story. If we are still living, there is hope for us yet. The loving-kindness of the Lord does not run out, and it won't pass over us. In life, in death, and in all things, there is hope for the redemption and restoration of things lost. Christ is our living hope, and he will not let us down.

Loving Lord, I am so thankful for your kindness that reaches deeper than I can fathom. Thank you for never giving up on me. I receive your love today as I turn my attention to worship you.

KINSMAN-REDEEMER

"Boaz is closely related to us. He is a kinsman-redeemer
of our family. May Yahweh greatly bless Boaz!"

RUTH 2:20

In Hebrew custom, if a widow was childless, a close male
relative was able and empowered to "redeem" her through
marriage and to buy back her property. This was a legal function
that served to ensure that the widow would not lose her
inheritance rights while also providing her with offspring.

Knowing that Boaz was a close relative, Naomi's hope soared
realizing that he was not only a generous man, but he could be
the one to redeem her line through uniting with Ruth. Christ is our
heavenly Kinsman-Redeemer. He set all wrong things right in our
relationship with the Father, giving us freedom in our identity in
him. He stepped in the gap and took all responsibility for us, and
he has become our covering. May we worship him for all that he
has done, is doing, and will continue to do in loyal loving-kindness.

*Jesus, you are my Redeemer and the restorer of all intended
inheritance in your kingdom. Thank you for the freedom and the
covering I have found in your love. I bind my heart and life to
yours forever, for you are generous and worthy.*

GRACIOUS GENEROSITY

Ruth the Moabite responded, "He even said to me,
'Stay close by my servants until they have finished all my harvest.'"

RUTH 2:21

*W*e cannot begin to exaggerate the grace and kindness of God. Just as Boaz went above and beyond in his generosity toward Ruth, so does Christ do the same with us. He does not simply allow us to glean from the leftovers of others, but he also sets out extra portions, along with allowing us the freedom to pick from stalks that were not ours to pick from. He is so very compassionate with us.

Will we take the invitation of Christ that welcomes us to stay close to his side? Will we stay near his fields, reaping the harvest from his kingdom, or will we go off on our own way to try and find something or someone better? We will not find a better or more generous King. The prodigal son learned that, and so will we if we choose to go off and then return. Let's stay close to the Lord, letting his love pour over us. He is wonderful and completely trustworthy.

Gracious King, I don't want to stray from you, for you are better than anyone I could ever pledge my life to. You are faithful, true, and full of mercy-kindness. I am yours.

ENCOURAGEMENT TO CONTINUE

Naomi replied, "It is best, my daughter, that you stay near his young women, otherwise you'll be alone and might be bothered in someone else's field."

RUTH 2:22

*N*aomi encouraged Ruth to keep returning to Boaz's field, as he had invited her to do. Her encouragement solidified the path that Ruth would take. Let us also share our opportunities with those who are trusted counselors in our lives. They may help us to gain confidence in stepping forward into new territories. Naomi knew that Ruth would probably not find such enormous favor with another field owner. And she knew not to pass up this opportunity.

When we allow others to speak into our lives, we get to lean on their wisdom, coupled with our own. We get their perspective that either confirms our direction or asks questions that help us to see other possibilities. May we not make decisions based on our own leanings, alone, when we have the fellowship of trusted friends, family, and counselors to weigh in. There, we will find encouragement and confidence when God's favor is clear.

Great God, thank you for setting me in close community. I know those I can trust to weigh in on my decisions. Thank you for both the encouragement and challenge I find in their wisdom.

FAITHFUL LOVE

Ruth worked alongside the young women who served Boaz. She lived with her mother-in-law and gleaned in Boaz's fields until the end of the barley and wheat harvests.

RUTH 2:23

*R*uth faithfully showed up to the fields day after day, doing the work that she was invited to do but also the work that needed to be done. She kept on living the normal day-to-day life of working, cooking, resting, and communing with her mother-in-law. Let's not gloss over the necessary faithfulness of showing up in the day-to-day, for that is where God meets us.

Beginnings are usually exciting, but as we get into the routine of long days, the novelty of God's favor at first may wear off with the exhaustion of the mundane. This is where we are refined in the faithful love of God. When we show up faithfully, we will reap the reward at the end of the harvest. Let us remember, in the ordinary and mundane of the everyday, that God's faithfulness is still at work.

Faithful One, thank you for the provision you have offered and for the partnership you have offered me in working hard. I am grateful for the safety and security of the routines of my life. Thank you!

DESIRE FOR MORE

One day, Naomi said to Ruth:
"I want to see you marry so that you'll be happy and secure."

RUTH 3:1

*N*aomi was well aware that Ruth was providing for them both, and she did not want to be a burden to Ruth's future prospects. She wanted Ruth to be able to marry again so that she could have the fulfillment of a happy marriage and family. She wanted that security for her, knowing the tumultuous state of being a widow herself.

We can desire more for ourselves, and we can desire more for others. Let's be encouragers of each other in faith and in life, pressing each other on in the pursuit of greater things. There is always more available to us spiritually in God's kingdom. There is often much more available to us in life if we will put ourselves in positions to push ahead. Is there an area that you have resisted though others have encouraged you toward it? Perhaps ask yourself whether the pushback is truly because you don't want it or for fear of disappointment or rejection. When we let fear rule our decisions, we limit ourselves. Love sets us free to dream big.

Lord, I trust you with my deep desires. Give me courage to walk ahead and do something about them.

REDEMPTIVE HOPE

"Now listen, a man named Boaz is our relative.
You worked with his servant girls in his fields.
This evening, he'll be winnowing barley on the threshing floor."

RUTH 3:2

*J*esus, our Kinsman-Redeemer, took every curse upon himself, along with our slavery to sin, when he clothed himself in flesh and blood. He entered into our experience so that he could step into the place of Redeemer. He is the appointed heir of all things, and he perpetuated the nature, character, and kingdom of God upon the earth in all that he did.

Just as Boaz was at the threshing floor winnowing his barley in the evening, Jesus is also at his threshing floor separating the chaff from the grain. He is doing the work that needs to be done after a great harvest has come in. May we find ourselves at his threshing floor, yielding to his mercy and to his gracious nature. He is our one true hope.

Redeemer, I come to you with all that I am, laying down my life, my expectations, and my will to you. Do with me what you will, for I have known you to be gracious and kind. I am yours.

ANOINT YOURSELF

"Now, take a bath and put on some nice perfume. Dress in your best clothes and go to the threshing floor, but don't let him know you're there until he's had plenty to eat and drink."

RUTH 3:3

Just as Ruth anointed herself before presenting herself before Boaz, may we also do the work of readying ourselves. We do this by being washed in the Word of God and by receiving the anointing of the Holy Spirit through prayer and devotion before the Lord. When we put on Christ, we are putting on our best clothes.

We have been perfected in the perfect righteousness of Jesus. We go down humbly to meet our beloved at his threshing room floor, where he waits for us. What a wonderful God he is that he provides everything we need to ready ourselves to fellowship with him. He is our covering, his truth is written upon our hearts through his living Word, and his Spirit is the anointing that gives off a sweet fragrance in his presence. Let's heed the advice of Naomi to Ruth and ready ourselves to meet our divine Kinsman-Redeemer.

Christ, thank you for clothing me with your love. I humbly offer you all that I have. I wash myself in your living Word and ready myself in the anointing oil of your presence.

RISK OF HUMILITY

"Watch closely to see where he lies down.
Then go, uncover his feet, and lie down there.
He will tell you what to do."

RUTH 3:4

The instructions that Naomi gave Ruth in going before Boaz were risky. She could have gone and followed everything to a tee and then found herself rejected and humiliated. If anyone saw her come to him, they both could have suffered the consequences of gossip and speculation. This was no small or easy task put before Ruth.

There will be times when vulnerability feels like the biggest risk we could take. It may feel safer to self-protect, but risk often brings with it the opportunity for a great reward. If Ruth had decided that it didn't feel worth it, she and Naomi could have still lived together, and Ruth could have continued to seek favor during other harvest seasons. But what of the time between harvests? She knew the risk, respected Naomi and her advice, and pushed through the potential fear of rejection. May we do the same. Our heavenly Boaz will instruct us, and all we need to do is listen and obey him.

Jesus, I humble myself before you and push through the fear that threatens to keep me small and stuck in cycles of lack. I trust you more than I want to remain comfortable.

May It Be

Ruth answered, "I'll do everything you've told me."

RUTH 3:5

*R*uth's answer to Naomi is humble acquiescence. She did not simply agree because she loved and respected her mother-in-law but because she also saw the benefit and reward of following through on her advice. When we are presented with situations that run high risks but also offer great rewards, may our faith and the encouragement of others propel us forward.

As we join our agreement with others and we welcome opportunities while trusting the faithfulness of God, we rest in the great company of faith. We do not go only for ourselves but for others. Often, the greatest risks we take in life will affect not only us but also those who could stand to benefit from them. May we take up the causes of the vulnerable and let our faith, coupled with theirs, push us ahead. In so doing, we will draw closer to the Lord, for he is our beloved One and the One to whom we go in all things.

Gracious One, I accept everything that you have for me, along with the courage it takes to move ahead in faith. I lean on your understanding above my own and partner with your purposes. You make me brave.

QUICK OBEDIENCE

That evening, Ruth went down to the threshing floor
and did all her mother-in-law had told her to do.

RUTH 3:6

*R*uth did not hem and haw after making the decision to follow Naomi's instructions. She went that very evening, quickly following the advice of her mother-in-law. She followed all the details that she had given her, and she followed through on her part.

May we be found as Ruth was, in quick and ready obedience to the instructions of the Lord. In Ruth's case, she had agreed to the advice of her mother-in-law. When we make agreements, it is important that we follow through on them in a timely manner. Though there are many responsibilities that we cannot shirk in this life, there is a way to prioritize the important ones so that we can be keepers of our word. May we be quick in fulfilling our part, and may we be swift in our obedience to the Lord.

Faithful One, thank you for the reminder of the importance of integrity. I lay down my excuses to put off what I know needs to be done for another day. Give me strength to follow through on all I said I would and give me wisdom in my commitments from here on out.

In the Details

> After his evening meal, Boaz was in a good mood. He went to
> lie down at the far end of the grain pile and fell fast asleep. Ruth
> quietly tiptoed over to him, uncovered his feet, and lay down.
>
> RUTH 3:7

*T*he detail of Naomi's instruction—even to the point of remarking that Ruth should wait until Boaz was in a good mood and had laid down—is remarkable. Why, I wonder, was it important that he be in a good mood? Perhaps if he had not been in a good mood, Ruth would have abandoned ship. But we know that was not how it played out, for he *was* in a good mood.

May we take the details of the Lord's instructions as seriously as Ruth did. He is a God of the details. When was the last time we felt pulled to a very specific route or way of doing things because of the leading of the Spirit? We should not be surprised when we are drawn to the specifics. Instead of brushing them off as silly, let's follow through on those inklings and see where they lead. We will find God's wisdom in the details of our stories, after all.

Sovereign Lord, thank you for being the God who shows up in detailed precision. Speak to me; I'm listening.

COURAGEOUS LOVE

Around midnight, Boaz was startled, and he awoke.
He was surprised to find a woman lying at his feet.

RUTH 3:8

Love is courageous. It takes risks, and it does not seek to control others. Here, Ruth's courage was not only about herself or Boaz, but it was also tied to her love and honor of Naomi. Boaz was startled to awake and find a woman lying at his feet. It makes sense that he was. He assumed he had been alone on the threshing floor. It was surprising to find at some point in the night that was no longer the case.

Ruth's courage and vulnerability was not a guarantee of Boaz's kind reception. She had known him to be a generous and honest man, but that did not mean she could foresee how he would respond to a strange woman lying at his feet. There is always a chance, when we act in vulnerability, that we will be wounded. However, courage does not require us to know the outcome; it simply requires us to act on it and face whatever comes.

Yahweh, I trust you with my future, and I trust your help in vulnerable situations. When I step out in courageous faith, you are my vision. Whatever comes, I know that you are with me.

December

TENDER APPEAL

"Who are you?" Boaz asked. "I am Ruth, your servant girl,"
she answered. "Spread the corner of your garment over me
because you are a close relative by marriage, one who is my
kinsman-redeemer."

RUTH 3:9

When Ruth asked Boaz to cover her with the corner of his
garment, she was in a sense asking him to marry her. She appealed
to the fact that he was her kinsman-redeemer and asked him to
show her the faithfulness to the covenant of Yahweh that she knew
him to portray in other areas of his life. It was both a vulnerable
and a tender appeal to his integrity, revealing her dependence on
his help.

When we come to the Lord, we ask him to spread the corner of his
garment over us. We humbly ask for his redemption to cover us.
And he does. He covers us with the faithfulness of his covenant,
and we are washed in the mercy of his kindness. May we never
hesitate from laying it all out before him, for he is our willing and
holy Redeemer.

*Redeemer, you are my greatest hope and the fulfillment of my
longings. I submit myself to your leadership and ask for your
mercy covering over my life. I am yours!*

LOVE'S KINDNESS

Boaz said: "Dear woman, may Yahweh bless you, for this act of kindness you are showing me exceeds the kindness you have shown to Naomi. You didn't search for a young man to marry, either rich or poor."

RUTH 3:10

*B*oaz's reply to Ruth's tender appeal is dripping with compassion, kindness, and humility. He recognized the honor of her request toward himself, for there were other men in the area who were younger that she could have appealed to. The vulnerability that they both displayed in this interaction is altogether beautiful and full of the mercy-heart of God.

The confidence of Ruth's plea, made from the strength of her identity, was sincere. Boaz's response was equally sincere. Love is kind, considerate, and full of courage. When we extend it from a pure place, making bold requests based in our identity but not seeking to control the other, we are reflecting the same kind of love Christ has toward us. May we all be as bold in love as Ruth was. May we also be as humble and kind in our loving responses as Boaz was to Ruth.

Lord, I want to walk in the strength and courage of your love in all that I do. Clothe me with your compassion and help me to let go of any need or desire to control another.

BEAUTIFUL RESPONSE

"My daughter, don't worry. I promise to do everything
you ask, because everyone knows you're a brave woman
of noble character."

RUTH 3:11

*R*uth's character was noble, and she was well-known for it. It was no secret that she had left her own homeland—including its culture, her family, and gods—and devoted herself to Naomi. She was respected for this decision, and she continually worked hard to provide for them both. She was virtuous, and she overcame the odds stacked against her as a widow and a foreigner. Loyal love and faithfulness will always yield good fruit.

Boaz's response to Ruth revealed the high esteem he held for her. He did not hold back his kindness nor did he leave her questioning his intentions. He was both clear and thoughtful. May we also communicate this way in our lives. Let us be crystal clear with our intentions and thoughtful in how we present them. Boaz already had the character and good reputation to back up his word. Let's make sure that our words and lives match up as well.

Faithful God, there is no one who speaks such tender words of love out of such purity of heart as you do. May I reflect you in my speech and in my life.

COMPLICATIONS ARISE

"It's true that I am a kinsman-redeemer,
but you have a closer kinsman-redeemer than I."

RUTH 3:12

Sometimes, when we are close to the breakthrough we've been waiting for in life, complications will arise. In Ruth and Boaz's case, it was a closer relative who could step in as kinsman-redeemer. For us, it may look like a stumbling block that we had not foreseen.

Boaz was a man of such honor and integrity that he would not make a promise he couldn't keep. He did, however, promise to follow through and help Ruth find her redeemer—whether it be himself or the other closer relative he mentioned. May we hold on to hope in the challenges that arise and trust, that no matter what, our Redeemer will take care of us. He is faithful, and he will make sure that we have the help we need for the breakthrough we have been longing for.

Redeemer, when challenges cause my heart to quake with worry, speak your words of truth to calm my soul. Fill me with your peace as I continue to trust in your unfailing love. No matter the details, I know that you will take care of me.

PROMISE OF REDEMPTION

"Stay here tonight, and I will protect you. In the morning,
we'll see if he's willing to redeem you. If he does, good; let him.
But if he refuses to redeem you, then I promise...I will."

RUTH 3:13

*B*oaz encouraged Ruth to stay under his protection through
the dark night. She rested at his feet until dawn came. In the dark
of night, Ruth could rest soundly under the promise that in the
morning, she would have a kinsman-redeemer.

Ruth rested under Boaz's watchful care, and we have an invitation
to rest under the protection of our Redeemer. In the unknowns
of how things will work out, we have no need to worry. God has
promised to offer us his redemption, and that is an eternal covering
for us. May we learn to rest in the peace of the presence of Jesus
who keeps watch over our souls. He will not let terror come to
us. He soothes our worried brows and quiets our souls with the
confident love he offers. He will not let us go, and he will follow
through on his promises.

*Jesus, I rest under the protection of your presence. Calm my
chaotic thoughts and turn my fears into fuel for faith, for I know
you are faithful and true.*

Awake with Wisdom

Ruth stayed near Boaz's feet that night.
She awoke before it was light enough for anyone to recognize her.

RUTH 3:14

*R*uth knew that in order to protect Boaz's, as well as her own, reputation, she needed to leave the threshing floor before it was light enough for anyone to recognize who she was. She took a risk in coming to him at all, but in the early morning hours, it was also still a risk to find her way home.

When we awake with wisdom, we know the steps we need to take. The Lord prepares us by speaking his instructions in his loving truth to our hearts. Let us heed his advice and be wise about how we go about our days. If we ignore his wisdom, we may face unnecessary consequences. If Ruth had slept longer, she may have been spotted, and perhaps the whole story of Ruth and Boaz would have turned out differently. Let's be wise and obedient, knowing the Lord directs us in his higher understanding.

Lord, help my heart to trust you so completely that I do not hesitate to act on your wisdom. I know that you see what I cannot and that you give direction with what is best for me, and for all, in mind. Thank you.

BEFORE YOU GO

As Ruth was about to leave, Boaz said to her,
"Here, bring me the cloak you're wearing and hold it open."

RUTH 3:15

When we are getting ready to embark on a faith journey, God does not leave us empty-handed. He calls us to him, and he gives us all that we need. In fact, he often gives so much more than we need in order to encourage our hearts in his faithfulness. His loyal love cannot be measured. The lengths of his grace, no one can gauge.

Before you go into your day, come to the Lord with open arms to receive what he has to offer you. There is always abundance in his presence, and his invitation is an open one for whenever you turn to him. There is no need to jump right into your day without coming to the Lord first. He knows what you need and, even more, what you long for. He will fill your cloak with the abundance of his peace, joy, love, and grace-strength. Come to him.

Faithful One, I come to you now, opening wide my arms to receive from the abundance of your love. Fill me with your life and encourage my heart in your nearness so that I may take that assurance into every place I enter today.

GENEROUS DETERMINATION

As she held it open, Boaz poured six measures of barley into it.
He then helped place it on her head to carry,
and she went back to Bethlehem.

RUTH 3:15

*T*hough we do not know exactly what measure Boaz used, we know that it was a generous amount that Ruth could carry herself. This remarkable amount of barley was to impress both Ruth and Naomi with Boaz's generosity and the determination he had to help them. It was like a seal of his promise, encouraging the women to trust that he would follow through on his word.

Jesus has given us more than enough to carry back to the people in our lives through the generosity of his presence. There is abundance in the fruit of his Spirit in our lives. There is love, joy, peace, patience, kindness, and self-control. There is hope, mercy, and power. He gives us not only what is sufficient to satisfy us but also a liberal portion to share with others. What a wonderfully bighearted God we have put our hope in. What a Redeemer!

Great God, thank you for the generosity of your heart. I receive all that you have to give, knowing that it is more than enough for me and mine. I trust you to work all things out in your mercy.

SHARE YOUR EXPERIENCE

When Ruth returned to her mother-in-law, Naomi asked her,
"How did it go, my dear daughter? How did Boaz receive you?"

RUTH 3:16

*W*hen we have had an encounter with the King of love, let us share with those close to us. When we share the generosity of God through the testimony of his goodness, others who also drink from his deep well of living water are likewise encouraged.

We don't need to shout from the rooftops our vulnerable experiences with the Lord, and often, it is wise to not do so. But we can and should share with those who understand, our close confidants and spiritual brothers and sisters. May we not hold back from sharing our victories, our breakthroughs, and the promises that also pertain to them. In this, we can celebrate together with the deep joy of answered prayers. When God gives us breakthrough, let's share it with those who have prayed with and for us, for it is their breakthrough and joy as well.

Faithful Father, thank you for your breakthrough power in the lives of those who look to you. I celebrate with those who are stepping into their promises fulfilled, and I will share my own answered prayers with those who will be encouraged as well.

MAGNANIMOUS MERCY

She added, "Boaz gave me all this barley, saying, 'You must not go
home empty-handed without a gift for your mother-in-law.'"

RUTH 3:17

The graciousness of Boaz did not simply extend to Ruth. He
went above and beyond, making sure that Naomi knew that the
generosity of his gift was for her as well. The mercy of God does
not simply affect us; it is extended to everyone in our lives. God's
mercy is not small nor is it small-minded. Its power spreads through
our connections with others and affects every aspect of them.

May we bring the gift of God's generous mercy into every one
of our relationships. There is love that abounds, hope that uplifts
us, and joy that runs deep. May we share the generous mercy of
God, the abundance of his love, and the overflow of his kingdom
with all those we interact with. There is more than enough to go
around.

*Gracious Lord, the abundance of your kingdom cannot be
exaggerated, and for that, I am so grateful. Broaden my
understanding and scope of your love as you pour it out in
overflowing measure so that I can bring it into every interaction I
have. Thank you!*

WAITING ON THE PROMISE

Naomi answered, "My daughter, wait here until you see what happens. Boaz will not rest until he has finished doing what he promised he would do."

RUTH 3:18

*T*here is always a space between a promise made and the fulfillment of it. In that waiting period, may we rest in the confident trust of the faithful One. Everything that he has vowed to do, he will do. His promises are sure, and he does not rest until each one is satisfied. Thankfully, he does not grow weary or tired, and he always finishes the work that he started.

As we wait on God, let's remember that Jesus finished all he needed to do to redeem us fully. We can rest in the working out of the details, for he has already done all that was required on our behalf. There is nothing that we can add to his goodness, and there is nothing that we can do to take away from the power of his mercy. His resurrection life is our own. His life in us awakens us to the liberty of his love. What a wonderful Savior.

Loving Lord, I rest in your finished work on the cross. My life is yours. Do what only you can do and bring the breakthrough I have been waiting for.

SEEING TO BUSINESS

No sooner had Boaz gone up to the city gate and sat down when the kinsman-redeemer of whom Boaz had spoken came passing by…"Come over here, friend…We have some business to attend to."

RUTH 4:1

*B*oaz did not waste any time in going to the city gate in order to do business with the kinsman-redeemer. He did not wait until later in the day or when it was more convenient for him. He went as soon as he could, and he took the steps to follow through quickly on the promise he made to Ruth.

Boaz did not know how the business dealing would go, whether the relative would accept his position as kinsman-redeemer or not. Yet, he did not hold back for fear of what the answer would be. May we have the same type of bold courage, knowing that even as we lay our hopes on the line, the whole truth must be presented. May we see to the business we have to do and not put it off for another moment, for there is no rest for us in the unanswered questions that we could have satisfied by doing what we know to do.

Great God, fill me with bold courage to do what needs to be done today. I trust you; I won't let fear stop me any longer.

GREATER MERCY

Then Boaz invited ten men of the city council and said,
"Please, sit down here with us."

RUTH 4:2

As Boaz invited ten members of the city council to sit down and witness the business that they were to attend to, he recognized the human responsibility of working out the question at hand. Though the law serves to add guilt to the human condition, including keeping Ruth out of the promise of Yahweh, Boaz revealed the greater mercy of God by doing for Ruth what no one else could do for her.

The mercy-heart of God does not exclude any who seek him. He welcomes all those who look to him. The mercy of God, as seen through Jesus, supersedes the laws set in place. The law of Christ's love is our measure in all things. We have been ushered into the kingdom of God with the redemptive love of Christ. There is nothing that the power of his death and resurrection leaves untouched. Though by human standards, we all have faults, Jesus has provided the redemption we need to be pure in his presence.

Messiah, thank you for providing a way to know you, to be claimed as your own, and to live under the covering of your mercy all the days of my life. You are a covenant-keeper, and for that, I am so grateful.

PRESENT WHAT IS OFFERED

Boaz turned to the kinsman-redeemer and said, "Sir, Naomi has returned from the country of Moab, and she's selling the piece of property that belonged to Elimelech."

RUTH 4:3

When Boaz presented the situation at hand to the kinsman-redeemer, he laid out the facts. He started at the beginning. When we present ourselves to others, whether we are looking to make a business deal or a friend, may we present ourselves with honesty and openness.

There is no reason to try to manipulate a situation by what we add or leave out. May we be transparent in our dealings, being full of integrity in all that we do. Let's not leave out important information, including the reason that brought us there to begin with, in the hope that they won't ask questions. With openness and honesty, we can clearly communicate what it is that we are offering. Who of us does not appreciate clarity?

Wise One, thank you for the clarity of your truth. I don't want to control others; I want to be clear and kind, just as Boaz was in his interactions. Help me to be open and to trust you with the unknowns.

OUGHT TO KNOW

"So I thought you ought to know about it. Buy it if you want...
As the kinsman-redeemer, you have the first right of refusal.
Redeem it if you choose to."

RUTH 4:4

*B*oaz would probably not have brought the issue of Naomi's selling her husband's land to the kinsman-redeemer if he had not had an interest in it. Knowing that he didn't lay first claim to it, however, he presented it to the kinsman-redeemer so that the other relative could make a choice. If he chose to buy the land, then Boaz could move on. If he chose not to, however, then Boaz could make the claim himself.

When we are presented with opportunities to help and yet know that there is someone else who is more apt to, what do we do? Do we follow the protocol and bring the matter to the attention of the person closer to the situation? When we do, we give them the chance to either take action or not, and then we can make our decision based off of that information. Boaz didn't bulldoze this situation, and we can follow his example.

God of order, thank you for the reminder that there is order to your kingdom. Where I have felt stuck, thank you for the perspective of your wisdom.

TRUE RESPONSIBILITY

"The day you buy the field from the hand of Naomi, you also acquire Ruth the Moabite, the widow of the dead...it will be your responsibility to father a child in order to maintain the dead man's name on his inheritance."

RUTH 4:5

*B*oaz mentioned the land before he mentioned Ruth. While the kinsman-redeemer was willing to buy the land, the responsibility of taking on Ruth as his wife was something he had to also consider. Boaz was willing to not only buy the land but also to pay the price to acquire both the field and the treasure.

This is reminiscent of the parable that Jesus told in Matthew 13. There, he described someone finding a treasure in a field. When he did, he sold all he had to buy that field, for he knew the true worth that was hidden there. Ruth was to Boaz a hidden treasure of great price. She was more than a responsibility; she was a fortune of much value to him.

Lord, thank you that I am more than a responsibility to care for. You value me more deeply than I can imagine. Through Boaz's actions, I see elements of your love for me. Thank you!

WEIGHTY MATTERS

At this, the kinsman-redeemer balked and said,
"In that case, I'm not able to redeem it for myself
without risking my own inheritance."

RUTH 4:6

When the kinsman-redeemer considered the cost of acquiring Ruth and the responsibility of giving her heirs, he decided it was too high a price to pay. In the same way, when we try to live up to the demands of the law, our response is "I can't do it." We are not able to pay the weighty price that the law requires. It is impossible for us.

Grace, however, is our hope of salvation—our only hope! The kinsman-redeemer rejected the opportunity in front of him in order to preserve his own name in Israel. However, his name has been lost. Boaz, in taking the place as kinsman-redeemer, not only allowed for Mahlon's line to continue, but he also preserved his own name. His name is recounted in this book, and it is read every year in Jewish celebrations. When we seek Yahweh's faithfulness, we receive an eternal name and are placed as pillars in the temple of our God.

Faithful One, I lay down my rights and take up your cause. Your faithfulness is all that matters, and I want to live according to the higher law of your love. I am yours!

RECEIVE YOUR RIGHTS

(At that time in Israel, in order to finalize a transaction concerning redeeming and transferring property, a man would customarily remove a sandal and give it to the other party, making the contract legally binding.)

RUTH 4:7

During this era in Israel, the sandal represented a man's property rights. When one gave up the sandal, it meant he would no longer walk on that property or claim it as his own. This symbolic gesture demonstrated the transferring of his rights to another.

When we stake our claim in the promises of God, we also receive something in the exchange. There is a yielding, a giving of authority from another that we accept as we obtain our rights to the territory. Let us not forget the importance of this interchange. When we acquire property today, there is an exchange of a deed. It gives us the authority we need to occupy the spaces we buy. Without that, we have no authority. So, let us be sure we have the proper representation we need to back up our claims.

Jesus, you have all authority over my life by your redemptive power. I receive all that you have to give, knowing that your authority is the only power I have to stand on.

Co-Heirs with Christ

When the kinsman-redeemer said to Boaz,
"Take my purchase option of redemption for yourself,"
he took off his sandal and gave it to Boaz.

RUTH 4:8

Jesus received the rights to surpass the law, and he obtained the promise of a more excellent ministry than the law offered. His ministry is one of reconciliation, and we are the joint heirs of his ministry. He has sown seeds of peace with God, and we reap the harvest of it. What a wonderful Savior! What an awesome Redeemer!

Let's receive the rights that Jesus offers us as his co-heirs. His law of love gives us authority to move in the power of his resurrection. We have come alive in his mercy, and we get to share with others the wonderful news of reconciliation with God. There is nothing that separates us from the fullness of God's kingdom in Christ, for our great Kinsman-Redeemer has laid claim to all that is his—and that includes us.

Redeemer, thank you for welcoming me into your family with the power of your mercy-kindness. I am submitted to you and your will. I walk in your authority, for I am yours.

PUBLIC WITNESS

Then Boaz turned to the elders and announced publicly, "Today, you are witnesses that I have purchased from the hand of Naomi all that belonged to Elimelech and all that belonged to Chilion and Mahlon."

RUTH 4:9

*T*here is something powerful in publicly declaring our faith. A marriage ceremony is a public declaration of love and devotion, often with many witnesses to celebrate the union. Baptisms, too, are events where our devotion to the Lord is noted and celebrated with others. Boaz publicly declared both his acquiring of Naomi's land and the intention to marry and care for Ruth.

There is accountability in our public statements. They are not frivolous desires or flimsy plans. They are our word and our intent. When we make big decisions in life where we will need the support and witness of others, let's not hold back from making them known. The witnesses will be able to back up what we said, to celebrate with us in our joy, and they will be able to hold us to our word.

Jesus, thank you for the strength in public witnesses with the important matters in life. I do not take it lightly. I will share my deep devotion and true intentions freely.

REDEEMING LOVE

"I have also acquired Ruth the Moabite, Mahlon's widow, to be my wife. I will raise children with her who will maintain the dead man's name on his inheritance so that the name of the dead may not be cut off...from his family line."

RUTH 4:10

*B*oaz's decision to marry Ruth would not only affect his household but also Naomi's. It was no small thing for him to step in as kinsman-redeemer. He vowed to give Ruth children and to raise them with her former husband's name so that Naomi's family line could continue. What a marvelously redemptive act this was. What merciful love.

Jesus is our ultimate Redeemer. He has vowed to love us, to bring us into his family, and to care for us from the abundance of his kingdom. Our fruitfulness in him is not just for his glory, but it is also a blessing to the generations that come after and through us. His redemptive love is sown into every part of our lives, and it will reap a bountiful harvest.

Redeemer, I can't begin to thank you for the ways your redemption power has changed me. I'm so grateful to know that it goes beyond my little life and that it will influence future generations.

LEAST BECOME GREATEST

Then all the elders and all the people...said: "We are witnesses.
May Yahweh make the woman who is coming into your house like
Rachel and Leah, both of whom built up the house of Israel."

RUTH 4:11

*I*n the response of the witnesses to Boaz's declaration, we see a generous blessing over Ruth. Though she was a foreigner, she was blessed as one of Israel's own. They prayed that Yahweh would bless her in the same way that he blessed Rachel and Leah—as those who were fruitful and multiplied their families and built up the house of Israel.

Though Ruth was a widow and a foreigner, she was covered by the redemptive power of Boaz's legacy. She went from being the least in the land to one of the greatest. Jesus does the same with each of us. No matter how we come to him—poor, needy, or vulnerable—God receives us and shelters us by giving us his name and welcoming us into his family. In Christ, those who seemed like they had nothing to offer become pillars of his mercy.

Faithful One, I am undone in the overflow of your mercy toward me. Thank you for being my covering and for calling me your own. How I love you!

EVEN MORE BLESSING

"May Yahweh give you children by this young woman,
and through them, may your family be like the family of Perez,
whom Tamar bore to Judah!"

RUTH 4:12

The people of Bethlehem were recalling a story of Yahweh's redemptive blessing toward Judah as they spoke over Naomi. Though Judah sinned, Yahweh turned that sin into goodness through his redemption. There is nothing in our lives, absolutely nothing, that cannot be redeemed by the Lord. This is great news for all of us who have carried shame.

Let's not hold anything back from Jesus. His redemptive love covers our disgrace, and he turns even our biggest mistakes into carriers of his glory. There is no need to hide from him, and there's nothing that surprises him. Let's yield our whole hearts, our whole lives, and all of our deeds and misdeeds to the power of Jesus' mercy. There, we will find even more blessing than we had hoped for.

Savior, thank you for the incomparable power of your love. There is nothing that you cannot do, and I trust your redemption to bring beauty out of the rubble of my mistakes. Do what only you can do and bring blessing where I could only see a curse.

TWO BECOME ONE

Boaz and Ruth married, and they became one as husband and wife. Yahweh opened Ruth's womb, and she bore a son.

RUTH 4:13

When two people marry, they become united in a deeply intimate way. No longer are they simply their own, but they become a unit. Just as Boaz and Ruth married and became one as husband and wife, when we unite our lives to the Lord in covenant, we enter into an intimate union with Jesus. We get to know his heart and his home in deeper ways. We join him in his purposes, and we partner with his power.

When we are united with the Lord, our lives will bear fruit. Ruth's womb was opened, and she bore a son. Our lives expand and promises are birthed through our union with Jesus. The fruit of our closeness with the Lord will be evident in our lives.

Jesus, thank you for your covenant with your people. Your bride is much larger than a person; it is your church. I want to know you deeply and to reflect your life in my own. I partner with you, knowing that my life is no longer my own. Your ways are better, and I choose to walk with you.

NEVER ABANDONED

The women of Bethlehem blessed Naomi:
"Praise Yahweh, who never abandoned you."

RUTH 4:14

*E*ven when Naomi was convinced that the Lord had utterly deserted her, he hadn't. In her overwhelming grief, she could not see any hopeful future or silver lining. She could not sense the nearness of Yahweh. Yet, the beautiful praise that the women of Bethlehem blessed Naomi with when Ruth bore a child was to proclaim that Yahweh had never abandoned her.

Never, not once, does God desert his people. Even when we don't know how to believe his goodness, he is still good. Even when we are walking on painful paths and we cannot see the redemption that the Lord is sowing, we can know that he is doing a good work. Praise Yahweh, who never ever abandons his people. Christ is the fullness of God in man. He is our hope, our Savior, and our companion. Through his Spirit, we know him and are fully known. We are never alone.

Christ, you are the perfect companion, never leaving or forsaking us. Thank you. I am overwhelmed by the goodness of your mercy that never lets up on my life. Be near and breathe hope where I have not yet known it.

FOREVER JOY

> "Praise Yahweh, who never...withheld from you a kinsman-redeemer! And may his name be famous in Israel!"
>
> RUTH 4:14

*T*he name of Boaz is remembered in the chronicles of Israel's history. His gracious act as kinsman-redeemer for Naomi and Ruth lives on as a beautiful picture of God's loving redemption. Nothing is wasted in the mercy of the Lord. Not a family goes unnoticed.

When we recount the story of Boaz and Ruth, it is a clear picture of Jesus' redemption of us. He offers us provision and protection. He gives us more than we could ask for. And when we request for the Lord's garment to cover us in covenant, he does it. Jesus paid the highest price so that we can be united with him in his kingdom, and our lives will bear eternal fruit. He is our forever joy and being welcomed into his family is our great reward.

Kinsman-Redeemer, you have done all that needed to be done so that I can be united with you. Your love didn't miss a single detail. I am completely yours, Lord! How deep my gratitude and joy go. Thank you.

RENEWED AND REFRESHED

"May this child renew your life and sustain you in your old age!
May your daughter-in-law, who loves you dearly, be more to you
than seven sons could ever be, for she has given you a wonderful
grandchild!"

RUTH 4:15

*C*hildren are a balm to the soul. The way they see the world so
innocently is refreshing. The purity of their joy is exuberant and
causes us to lighten up too. Whether we have children of our own
or not, we can learn beautiful lessons from them. Jesus welcomed
the little children to come to him. He encouraged everyone to have
the same pure faith as a child, letting wonder lead us to his heart.

Naomi was refreshed in more than one way through her grandson.
He was the product of the faithful redemption of God in her
life. He was a gift to her hope and a restoration to her identity.
She was no longer the bitter Marah as her life was transformed
with his own, and she reflected the meaning of her name once
more: "pleasant." Her life had become pleasant in the redemptive
renewal of God's favor.

*Faithful Father, thank you for the refreshing I find in your
presence. Sustain me and make me new in your fresh mercy.*

FROM DESPAIR TO DELIGHT

Naomi took her grandson and cuddled him in her arms
and cared for him as if he were her own.

RUTH 4:16

*F*rom the beginning of the story of Ruth to the end, we see a transformation, not only in Naomi's circumstances, but also in her heart. When she first left Moab, she was filled with despair. She had no hope, no joy, and no peace. She was broken down by the tragedy of her grief.

We watched her spirits transform as she realized that Boaz was a kinsman-redeemer and that he favored Ruth. Surely, her heart began to hope when Ruth brought home the abundant grain that Ruth had worked for, as well as what Boaz had gifted to her. She began to believe again in the goodness of God. When we live through hard times when we cannot see any bit of hope, let's take encouragement from Naomi's transformation. All things are made new in the redemptive love of Christ. He takes our despair, and he sows seeds of delight.

Wonderful One, thank you for the encouragement of your liberating love. Fill me with hope as I look to you for my breakthrough. I believe that you aren't finished with me yet.

RESTORED HOPE

The women of the neighborhood gave him a name, saying,
"At last, Naomi has a son!"

RUTH 4:17

*T*he name that was given to Naomi's grandson was *Obed*. This means "worshiper" or "servant [of Yahweh]." He was a gift from God, and his life was an offering of worship to the Lord. This is reminiscent of the great love of God. We love because he first loved us. He provides for us, and we offer a portion back to him in worship.

Though Naomi had lost her sons, Obed became like a son to her. He was more than a grandchild; he was the promise that her line would not end. As sons carried on their family names, so did Obed carry Naomi's name on. What a beautifully restored hope this was. How overwhelmingly grateful must she have felt in knowing that God's faithfulness meant the continuation of her family line. We can take heart from Naomi's story. Even in the most impossible places, God can restore our hope and bring life out of the ashes of our deep disappointment.

Gracious Lord, there is no one who can do what you can. Your mercy restores even the most shattered hopes. Your love lifts us up and renews our joy. Show me where you are doing this, even now in my life.

GENEALOGY OF JESUS

They named him Obed,
and he became the father of Jesse,
the father of David.

RUTH 4:17

*N*ot only does the story of Ruth end in redemption, but it also leads us to the genealogy of the Messiah. Ruth, though she was a foreigner in Israel, became the father of Obed, who became the father of Jesse, who was the father of King David.

Let us never mistake the power of God's redemption. Its mark goes far beyond our own little lives and reaches into the destinies of others. Ruth's obedience became her legacy, and her family line led to David, which eventually led to Jesus. What an enormous honor. May we live our lives with abandon, pursuing excellence and integrity as we walk the path of Christ's love. As we do, he will multiply our efforts and his glory will be made known through the generations that follow.

Gracious Jesus, I trust you to guide me as I look to you. I know that you will do far more than I can ever comprehend in the unmistakable power of your love. You are glorious, and I worship you with my life.

OUTSIDERS BECOME INSIDERS

Boaz the father of Obed, Obed the father of Jesse,
who had a famous son, King David.

RUTH 4:21–22

One thing that we can unmistakably take from the story of Ruth is that no one is an outsider in the kingdom of God. When we submit our lives to the loving lead of the Lord, we become his own. We are as dear to him as Abraham, Moses, David, or Peter. The Father sees us through Jesus. His affection for us is as pure as it is for his own Son.

Jesus went to the margins when he walked the earth, ministering to the hurting, the broken, and the outcast. He invited the dregs of society to know the powerful mercy-love of God the Father. He made it clear that everyone is welcome in his Father's house. May we follow his lead, not judging others on their appearance or shutting people out because of their status. Let's be a people of welcome, for there are no outsiders in God's kingdom. All who are hungry and all who are thirsty will eat, drink, and be satisfied when they come to him.

Merciful King, thank you for your lavish love that welcomes us in and never pushes us away. Help me to be like you in mercy-kindness. I love you.

About the Author

BRIAN SIMMONS is the lead translator of The Passion Translation®. The Passion Translation (TPT) is a heart-level translation that uses Hebrew, Greek, and Aramaic manuscripts to express God's fiery heart of love to this generation, merging the emotion and life-changing truth of God's Word. The hope for TPT is to trigger inside every reader an overwhelming response to the truth of the Bible and to reveal the deep mysteries of the Scriptures in the love language of God, the language of the heart. Brian is currently translating the Old Testament.

After a dramatic conversion to Christ in 1971, Brian and his wife, Candice, answered the call of God to leave everything behind and become missionaries to unreached peoples. Taking their three children to the tropical rain forest of Central America, they planted churches for many years with the Paya-Kuna people group. Brian established leadership for the churches that Jesus birthed and, having been trained in linguistics and Bible translation principles, assisted with the translation of the Paya-Kuna New Testament.

After their ministry overseas, Brian and Candice returned to North America, where Brian began to passionately work toward helping people encounter the risen Christ. He and his wife planted numerous ministries, including a dynamic church in New England (US). They also established Passion & Fire Ministries, under which they travel full time as Bible teachers in service of local churches throughout the world.

Brian is the author of numerous books, Bible studies, and devotionals that help readers encounter God's heart and experience a deeper revelation of God as our Bridegroom King, including *Throne Room Prayer, The Sacred Journey, Prayers on Fire, The Divine Romance,* and *The Vision.*

Brian and Candice have been married since 1971 and have three children as well as precious grandchildren and great-grandchildren. Their passion is to live as loving examples of a spiritual father and mother to this generation.